VB.NET

Common Ground

Richard Thomas Edwards

The terms I live by

Wax on, wax of

When everything depends on flexibility, depend on this.
—Richard Thomas Edwards

Good morning, good afternoon, or good evening. Welcome to my world. I wish I could last forever and not have to worry about the biological ticking time bomb that my body came with as part of the package of human awareness, but I don't.

Be glad I know I do. Otherwise, I'd most likely spend the next ten years writing 5000 books on why the world is not flat, and such trivial nonsense that even I would have to be sedated, chained to a chair and be forced to read such nonsense.

Besides, lucky for you, I hate long dissertations and make assumptions that you already have a good grasp on VB.Net and its massive power. Okay, massive might be a bit strong. Never-the-less, it still has a lot of punch.

Do it and learn it

Right off the bat, we must establish an agreement with each other. To learn how to do something, you have to repeat the process otherwise, it doesn't stay with you. Did you comfortably learn how to tie your shoes without repetition, or ride a bicycle without it?

If course not. So, don't expect expertise to be handed over to you on a silver platter. Besides, if you really want to land a job in IT, you're going to be going up to a white board and showing a perspective employer that you know your stuff.

Technical terms are not as important as understand execution

I can't tell you how important being able to write the code is verses being able to spit out tech jargon is. In fact, I have landed more jobs being able to show perspective employers that I knew the way I would solve their issues on the white board over trying to explain, in technical terms, how I would resolve it.

Actions do speak louder than words.

Of course, there are those however moments. And we're about to cover one of those in the next chapter.

Binding Basics
The devil is in the details

One of the first questions asked of an entry level programmer regarding Visual Basic in general and VB.Net in particular: What are the three kinds of bindings?

The quick answer is: Early, mixed and late. The long answer is:

In early binding, we make a reference to a namespace, use the Imports statement at the very top of the class and then bask in the behind the scenes program's ability to provide us with suggestions on how to write the code.

Mixed Binding, we perform the same steps but use CreateObject or GetObject to instantiate the object at runtime. Gives us the ability to do what we have to do in the IDE but not depend on the object being the same version we used on other machines.

Basically, how we got around the infamous "dll hell".

Late binding doesn't use a reference or an imports statement but relies on the programmer to know enough about the objects being used to create them and perform all the necessary actions to write the code without the help of the program that assists with code complete.

Whose writing what and when
The practice of understanding the code logic

If someone asked me what time it is, I could be a wise guy and say: a few seconds after you asked me that, now when I'm responding and after you heard my response.

Of course, that wasn't what the person asking me really wanted to hear and I might not like the incoming round to my jaw for being a wise guy, but in fact, it is the truth.

However, in the world of programming, the three basic modes of when something happens is more specific and precise.

Written Now, is the concept that when you write code, you want the code to execute immediately.

Written Interactively, means when the code is written, it is written to be run on demand but also supplies the external program with specific details that can be counted on and not written that way without the support.

A perfect example of this is when you want to provide the external program with the correct connection string and\or query for another programming language that you have created with your code.

Written at runtime means your program is producing something that will stand on its own two feet and work independently of your program.

The last two are generally written to a file.

VB.Net does Access

And DAO

Access is not DAO and DAO is not Access. Access uses DAO to create databases, create and populate tables and return Recordsets either through direct access to them or by calling QueryDefs or stored procedures.

Beyond that Access is very similar to VB6 in that you can create forms, modules and classes that enable users to visually see what they need to see and work with information in ways that that are unique to the product. It also uses its own form of visual basic called VBA or Visual Basic For Applications.

We will cover DAO in more detail in the chapter on DAO. Right now, here's some good to know information:

There four versions of database files you can create through automation:

1. oAccess.NewCurrentDatabase("C:\test\Myfirst.mdb", 9) --2000
2. oAccess.NewCurrentDatabase("C:\test\Myfirst.mdb", 10) --2003
3. oAccess.NewCurrentDatabase("C:\test\Myfirst.accdb", 12) -- 2007
4. oAccess.NewCurrentDatabase("C:\test\Myfirst.accdb", 0) --Default

There are two file types of Access Database extensions, as shown below:

1. oAccess.OpenCurrentDatabase("C:\test\Myfirst.mdb")
2. oAccess.OpenCurrentDatabase ("C:\test\Myfirst.accdb")

Take a look at the code below and remember, WbemScripting is not the only engine that can create and populate an Access Database. Everything in this book can. Even Access itself.

```
Dim ns As String = "root\cimv2"
Dim Classname As String = "Win32_Process"
strQuery = "Select * From " & Classname
objs = GetObject("Winmgmts:\\.\" & ns).ExecQuery(strQuery)

Dim db As Object = Nothing
Dim oAccess As Object = CreateObject("Access.Application")
Dim fso As Object = CreateObject("Scripting.FileSystemObject")
If fso.FileExists(Application.StartupPath & "\" + Classname + ".mdb") = True Then
    oAccess.OpenCurrentDatabase(Application.StartupPath & "\" + Classname + ".mdb")
    db = oAccess.CurrentDB
Else
    oAccess.NewCurrentDatabase(Application.StartupPath & "\" + Classname + ".mdb", 10)
    db = oAccess.CurrentDB
End If


Dim tbldef As Object = db.CreateTableDef(Classname & "_Properties")

For Each obj In objs
    For Each prop In obj.Properties_
        Dim fld As Object = tbldef.CreateField(prop.Name, 12)
        fld.AllowZeroLength = True
        tbldef.Fields.Append(fld)
    Next
    Exit For
Next

db.TableDefs.Append(tbldef)


Dim rs As Object = db.OpenRecordset(Classname & "_Properties")

For Each obj In objs
    rs.AddNew()
    For Each prop In obj.Properties_
        rs.Fields(prop.Name).Value = GetValue(prop.Name, obj)
    Next
    rs.Update()
Next
```

With or without the use of WMI, the basic functionality of the code is undisputable.

Create or open a database. Wire a DAO Database to the current database. Create a new TableDef and name it, add fields to it, append the new fields to the new TableDef and then append the new TableDef to the Database.

Then open the new TableDef as a recordset and populate it by doing a rs.AddNew() before each column is filled and using an rs.Update() until all the column values have been added to the table.

For certain, if this is the only thing I'm doing with Access, I certainly don't need Access to this.

VB.Net does ADO

And other side dishes

ADO is an acronym for Active-X Data Objects. In VBSCRIPT, you can use it to connect to both the 32-bit and 64-bit versions of Providers, Drivers and ISAMS

The reason why ADO came about in the first place was because DAO relied a lot on disk drives to do most of the work and disk drives were extremely slow.

It is also what was used to build the .Net ODBC, OLEDB, Oracle Client and SQL Client components. So, everything you do in ADO can be applied to the various .Net world as well. Therefore, if you learn ADO, the others are self-explanatory and a walk in the park.

This toolkit includes:

- ADODB.Connection
- ADODB.Command
- ADODB.RecordSet

While I love working with SQL Server, I use it in its simplest of terms. I create a connection string cnstr and then a strQuery as my SQL query string.

Here' how these combinations have been worked with in the past:

- Connection, Command and Recordset
- Connection and Recordset
- Command and Recordset
- Recordset

Most of my experiences deal with these four conventions although I have used the ADODB.STREAM with XML and ADSI.

Below are what you will see when these are combined:

```
Dim cn As Object = CreateObject("Adodb.Connection")
Dim cmd As Object = CreateObject("Adodb.Command")
Dim rs As Object = CreateObject("Adodb.Recordset")

cn.ConnectionString = cnstr
cn.Open()

cmd.ActiveConnection = cn
cmd.CommandType = 1
cmd.CommandText = strQuery
rs = cmd.Execute()
```

Okay so, what is this used for? This code example is used to produce a forward only recordset. It is fast. But you can't use it for adding additional rows or perform edits and updates.

If you want a more robust coding scenario, you'll want to use the connection and Recordset combination or just the recordset. However, the combination of all three can produce a RecordCount which can be used for adding records and editing and updating columns.

```
Dim cn As Object = CreateObject("Adodb.Connection")
cmd As Object = CreateObject("Adodb.Command")
Dim rs As Object = CreateObject("Adodb.Recordset")

cn.ConnectionString = cnstr
cn.Open()

cmd.ActiveConnection = cn
cmd.CommandType = 1
cmd.CommandText = strQuery
cmd.Execute()

rs.ActiveConnection = cn
rs.Cursorlocation = 3
rs.Locktype = 3
```

```
rs.Open(cmd)
```

Now, you can get the RecordCount and do AddNew, edit, delete and updates on the table.

Connection And Recordset

```
Dim cn As Object = CreateObject("Adodb.Connection")
Dim rs As Object = CreateObject("Adodb.Recordset")
cn.ConnectionString = cnstr
cn.Open()

rs.ActiveConnection = cn
rs.Cursorlocation = 3
rs.Locktype = 3
rs.Source = strQuery
rs.Open()
```

Again, you can get the RecordCount and do AddNew, edit, delete and updates on the table

Command And Recordset

```
Dim cmd As Object = CreateObject("Adodb.Command")
Dim rs As Object = CreateObject("Adodb.Recordset")
cmd.ActiveConnection = cnstr
cmd.CommandType = 1
cmd.CommandText = strQuery
rs = cmd.Execute()
```

Or

```
cmd.Execute()
rs.Cursorlocation = 3
rs.Locktype = 3
rs.Open(cmd)
```

Now, you can get the RecordCount and do AddNew, edit, delete and updates on the table.

Recordset

```
Dim rs As Object = CreateObject("Adodb.Recordset")
rs.ActiveConnection = cnstr
rs.Cursorlocation = 3
rs.Locktype = 3
rs.Source = strQuery
rs.Open()
```

VB.Net does ADO ISAMs
The legacy of a dying breed

In plain English, it is a text file. The idea was to take a folder and it a database and then take a file and it a table. Similar to the way JSOM works.

One of the biggest issues – and one that brought smiles to our technical support faces – was to explain, politely to our customers that the reason why they were getting an error when they tried to create a database was the fact that the folder already existed.

Every text file you create will have some kind of delimiter. Otherwise, placing information into a text file would be just another text file and you couldn't reuse the information because there would be nothing a program – including ours – could use to separate one field from another.

These are all various files we're going to be covering, so they really don't change that much. But they are used quite often as data storage and data files.

Of course, CSV or coma delimited is just one of dozens of possibilities. And all of these are fairly easy to code. You enumerate through strNames and StrValues and then add the delimiter of choice to separate the fields.

Problem is, it doesn't work. At least, not yet. It will soon. In fact, after I get done with it, you are going to become a master of Delimited files.

ISAMS USED WITH Microsoft.Jet.OLEDB.4.0

ISAM	Is The Folder	Is	The	File	Are	Tables
Engine	Path	The	Name		The	Internal

	Database	Database	
dBase 5.0	Yes	No	No
dBase III	Yes	No	No
dBase IV	Yes	No	No
Excel 3.0	No	Yes	Yes
Excel 4.0	No	Yes	Yes
Excel 5.0	No	Yes	Yes
Excel 8.0	No	Yes	Yes
HTML Export	No	Yes	Yes
HTML Import	No	Yes	Yes
Jet 2.x	No	Yes	Yes
Lotus WJ2	Yes	No	No
Lotus WJ3	Yes	No	No
Lotus WK1	Yes	No	No
Lotus WK3	Yes	No	No
Lotus WK4	Yes	No	No
Paradox	Yes	No	No

3.X			
Paradox	Yes	No	No
4.X			
Paradox	Yes	No	No
5.X			
Text	No	No	No

Basically, the rule of thumb here is if it isn't a Microsoft product, the Database if the folder and the file is the table.

VB.Net Creates ISAM Files

Your guess is a good as mine as to just how long that lasts

Below are examples on how to create them:

```
Dim cnstr As String
cnstr  = "Provider=Microsoft.OleDb.4.0; Data Source = C:\Program Files
(x86)\Microsoft Visual Studio\vb98\nwind.mdb;"
Dim cn as Adodb.Connection = new ADODB.Connection
cn.ConnectionString = cnstr
cn.Open()
```

CSV

```
Cn.Execute("Select * INTO [text; hdr=yes; database=" &
Application.StartupPath & "\].[" & Classname & ".csv] From [" & Classname & "]")
```

dBase III

```
Cn.Execute("Select * INTO [dBase III; hdr=yes; database=" &
Application.StartupPath & "\].[" & Classname & ".dbf] From [" & Classname & "]")
```

dBase IV

```
Cn.Execute("Select * INTO [dBase IV; hdr=yes; database=" &
Application.StartupPath & "\].[" & Classname & ".dbf] From [" & Classname & "]")
```

dBase 5.0

```
Cn.Execute("Select * INTO [dBase 5.0; hdr=yes; database=" &
Application.StartupPath & "\].[" & Classname & ".dbf] From [" & Classname & "]")
```

Excel 3.0

```
Cn.Execute("Select * INTO [Excel 3.0;hdr=yes; database=" &
Application.StartupPath & "\].[" & Classname & ".xls] From [" & Classname & "]")
```

Excel 4.0

```
Cn.Execute("Select * INTO [Excel 4.0;hdr=yes; database=" &
Application.StartupPath & "\].[" & Classname & ".xls] From [" & Classname & "]")
```

Excel 5.0

```
Cn.Execute("Select * INTO [Excel 5.0;hdr=yes; database=" &
Application.StartupPath & "\].[" & Classname & ".xls] From [" & Classname & "]")
```

Excel 8.0

```
Cn.Execute("Select * INTO [Excel 8.0;hdr=yes; database=" &
Application.StartupPath & "\].[" & Classname & ".xls] From [" & Classname & "]")
```

HTML Export

```
Cn.Execute("Select * INTO [HTML Export; hdr=yes; database=" &
Application.StartupPath & "\].[" & Classname & ".html] From [" & Classname & "]")
```

Lotus WJ2

```
Cn.Execute("Select * INTO [Lotus WJ2;hdr=yes; database=" &
Application.StartupPath & "\].[" & Classname & ".wj2] From [" & Classname & "]")
```

Lotus WJ3

```
Cn.Execute("Select * INTO [Lotus WJ3;hdr=yes; database=" &
Application.StartupPath & "\].[" & Classname & ".wj3] From [" & Classname & "]"
```

Lotus WK1

```
Cn.Execute("Select * INTO [Lotus WK1;hdr=yes; database=" &
Application.StartupPath & "\].[" & Classname & ".wk1] From [" & Classname & "]")
```

Lotus WK3

```
Cn.Execute("Select * INTO [Lotus WK2;hdr=yes; database=" &
Application.StartupPath & "\].[" & Classname & ".wk3] From [" & Classname & "]")
```

Lotus WK4

```
Cn.Execute("Select * INTO [dBase WK4;hdr=yes; database=" &
Application.StartupPath & "\].[" & Classname & ".wk4] From [" & Classname & "]")
```

Paradox 3.x

```
Cn.Execute("Select * INTO [Paradox 3.x;hdr=yes; database=" &
Application.StartupPath & "\].[" & Classname & ".db] From [" & Classname & "]")
```

Paradox 4.x

```
Cn.Execute("Select * INTO [Paradox 4.x;hdr=yes; database=" &
Application.StartupPath & "\].[" & Classname & ".db] From [" & Classname & "]")
```

Paradox 5.x

```
Cn.Execute("Select * INTO [Paradox 5.x;hdr=yes; database=" &
Application.StartupPath & "\].[" & Classname & ".db] From [" & Classname & "]")
```

Paradox 7.x

```
Cn.Execute("Select * INTO [Paradox 7.x;hdr=yes; database=" &
Application.StartupPath & "\].[" & Classname & ".db] From [" & Classname & "]")
```

Text

```
Cn.Execute("Select * INTO [text; hdr=yes; database=" & Application.StartupPath
& "\].[" & Classname & ".txt] From [" & Classname & "]")
```

About Text custom delimiter File Issues

There were a lot of news group conversations about and little resolve of an issue that involved the subject of the use of custom delimiters such as the tilde. Well, the resolution requires the following steps:

Use the creation code above. Go to the location of the file, open the Schema file created in the same folder, look for the name of the text file you created, change the Format=CSVDelimited entry to Format = Delimited(~). Close the file. Delete the text file, run:

```
Cn.Execute("Select * INTO [text; hdr=yes; database=" &
Application.StartupPath & "\].[" & Classname & ".txt] From [" & Classname & "]")
```

Open the newly created file and it will be tilde delimited.

VB.Net Opens ISAM Files

If you create them, you can use them

The secret here is with Extended Properties. While the cn.ConnectionString can be used, it is much easier and cleaner looking to do this:

```
Dim cn as ADODB.Connection = new ADODB.Connection
cn.Provider = "Microsoft.Jet.OleDb.4.0"
cn.Properties("Extended Properties").Value = "dBase III; hdr=yes;"
cn.Properties("Data Source").Value = Path
cn.Open()
```

The code below assumes the database path and the table name is passed in as part of the connection options.

```
Dim cn As Object = CreateObject("ADODB.Connection")
```

CSV

```
cn.ConnectionString = "Provider=Microsoft.Jet.OleDb.4.0; Extended
Properties=""text; hdr=yes;""; Data Source=" & dbpath & ";"
```

dBase III

```
cn.ConnectionString = "Provider=Microsoft.Jet.OleDb.4.0; Extended
Properties=""dBase III; hdr=yes;""; Data Source=" & dbpath & ";"
```

dBase IV

```
cn.ConnectionString = "Provider=Microsoft.Jet.OleDb.4.0; Extended
Properties=""dBase IV; hdr=yes;"""; Data Source=" & dbpath & ";"
```

dBase 5.0

```
cn.ConnectionString = "Provider=Microsoft.Jet.OleDb.4.0; Extended
Properties=""dBase 5.0; hdr=yes;"""; Data Source=" & dbpath & ";"
```

Excel 3.0

```
cn.ConnectionString = "Provider=Microsoft.Jet.OleDb.4.0; Extended
Properties=""Excel 3.0; hdr=yes;"""; Data Source=" & dbpath & "\" &
dbName & ";"
```

Excel 4.0

```
cn.ConnectionString = "Provider=Microsoft.Jet.OleDb.4.0; Extended
Properties=""Excel 4.0; hdr=yes;"""; Data Source=" & dbpath & "\" &
dbName & ";"
```

Excel 5.0

```
cn.ConnectionString = "Provider=Microsoft.Jet.OleDb.4.0; Extended
Properties=""Excel 5.0; hdr=yes;"""; Data Source=" & dbpath & "\" &
dbName & ";"
```

Excel 8.0

```
    cn.ConnectionString = "Provider=Microsoft.Jet.OleDb.4.0; Extended
Properties=""Excel 6.0; hdr=yes;""; Data Source=" & dbpath & "\" &
dbName & ";"
```

HTML Import

```
    cn.ConnectionString = "Provider=Microsoft.Jet.OleDb.4.0; Extended
Properties=""HTML Import; hdr=yes;"";Data Source=" & dbpath &
"\" & dbName & ";"
```

Lotus WJ2

```
    cn.ConnectionString = "Provider=Microsoft.Jet.OleDb.4.0; Extended
Properties=""Lotus WJ2; hdr=yes;""; Data Source=" & dbpath & "\" &
dbName & ";"
```

Lotus WJ3

```
    cn.ConnectionString = "Provider=Microsoft.Jet.OleDb.4.0; Extended
Properties=""Lotus WJ3;hdr=yes;""; Data Source=" & dbpath & "\" &
dbName & ";"
```

Lotus WK1

```
    cn.ConnectionString = "Provider=Microsoft.Jet.OleDb.4.0; Extended
Properties=""Lotus WK1;hdr=yes;""; Data Source=" & dbpath & "\" &
dbName & ";"
```

Lotus WK3

cn.ConnectionString = "Provider=Microsoft.Jet.OleDb.4.0; Extended Properties=""Lotus WK3;hdr=yes;"""; Data Source=" & dbpath & "\" & dbName & ";"

Lotus WK4

cn.ConnectionString = "Provider=Microsoft.Jet.OleDb.4.0; Extended Properties=""Lotus WK4;hdr=yes;"""; Data Source=" & dbpath & "\" & dbName & ";"

Paradox 3.X

cn.ConnectionString = "Provider=Microsoft.Jet.OleDb.4.0; Extended Properties=""Paradox 3.X; hdr=yes;"""; Data Source=" & dbpath & ";"

Paradox 4.X

cn.ConnectionString = "Provider=Microsoft.Jet.OleDb.4.0; Extended Properties=""Paradox 4.X; hdr=yes;"""; Data Source=" & dbpath & ";"

Paradox 5.X

cn.ConnectionString = "Provider=Microsoft.Jet.OleDb.4.0; Extended Properties=""Paradox 5.X; hdr=yes;"""; Data Source=" & dbpath & ";"

Paradox 7.X

```
cn.ConnectionString = "Provider=Microsoft.Jet.OleDb.4.0; Extended Properties=""Paradox 7.X; hdr=yes;""; Data Source=" & dbpath & ";"
```

Text

```
cn.ConnectionString = "Provider=Microsoft.Jet.OleDb.4.0; Extended Properties=""Text; hdr=yes;""; Data Source=" & dbpath & ";"
```

VB.Net does ADO and a Dataset
Shocking, simply shocking

Unless you are anal about datatypes, not only can you convert your ADO Recordset to a DataSet, you can do the same with the DataTable and the DataView.

```
Public Class Form1

    Private Sub Form1_Load(sender As System.Object, e As
System.EventArgs) Handles MyBase.Load
        Dim cn As Object = CreateObject("ADODB.Connection")
        cn.Provider = "Microsoft.Jet.OleDb.4.0"
        cn.Properties("Extended Properties").Value = "text;
hdr=yes;"
        cn.Properties("Data Source").Value = "C:\"
        cn.Open()

        Dim rs As Object = CreateObject("ADODB.Recordset")
        rs.ActiveConnection = cn
        rs.CursorLocation = 3
        rs.Locktype = 3
        rs.Source = "Select * from [Products.csv]"
        rs.Open()

        Dim ds As New System.Data.DataSet
        Dim dt As New System.Data.DataTable
        ds.Tables.Add(dt)
```

```vb
        For x As Integer = 0 To rs.Fields.Count - 1
            ds.Tables(0).Columns.Add(rs.Fields(x).Name)
        Next

        rs.MoveFirst()

        Do While rs.EOF = False
            Dim dr As System.Data.DataRow = ds.Tables(0).NewRow
            For x As Integer = 0 To rs.Fields.Count - 1
                dr.Item(rs.Fields(x).Name) = rs.Fields(x).Value
            Next
            ds.Tables(0).Rows.Add(dr)
            rs.MoveNext()
        Loop

        DataGridView1.DataSource = ds.Tables(0)

    End Sub

End Class
```

This results in:

ProductID	ProductName	SupplierID	CategoryID	QuantityPerUnit	UnitPrice	UnitsInStock	UnitsOnOrder	ReorderLevel	Discontinued
1	Chai	1	1	10 boxes x 20 bags	18	39	0	10	False
2	Chang	1	1	24 - 12 oz bottles	19	17	40	25	False
3	Aniseed Syrup	1	2	12 - 550 ml bottles	10	13	70	25	False
4	Chef Anton's Cajun Seasoning	2	2	48 - 6 oz jars	22	53	0	0	False
5	Chef Anton's Gumbo Mix	2	2	36 boxes	21.35	0	0	0	True
6	Grandma's Boysenberry Spread	3	2	12 - 8 oz jars	25	120	0	25	False
7	Uncle Bob's Organic Dried Pears	3	7	12 - 1 lb pkgs.	30	15	0	10	False
8	Northwoods Cranberry Sauce	3	2	12 - 12 oz jars	40	6	0	0	False
9	Mishi Kobe Niku	4	6	18 - 500 g pkgs.	97	29	0	0	True
10	Ikura	4	8	12 - 200 ml jars	31	31	0	0	False
11	Queso Cabrales	5	4	1 kg pkg.	21	22	30	30	False
12	Queso Manchego La Pastora	5	4	10 - 500 g pkgs.	38	86	0	0	False
13	Konbu	6	8	2 kg box	6	24	0	5	False

VB.Net does ADO and a Datatable

Just when you thought you've see it all

This is going to sound like a broken record. Unless you are anal about datatypes, not only can you convert your ADO Recordset to a DataTable.

```vb
Public Class Form1

    Private Sub Form1_Load(sender As System.Object, e As System.EventArgs) Handles MyBase.Load
        Dim cn As Object = CreateObject("ADODB.Connection")
        cn.Provider = "Microsoft.Jet.OleDb.4.0"
        cn.Properties("Extended Properties").Value = "text; hdr=yes;"
        cn.Properties("Data Source").Value = "C:\"
        cn.Open()

        Dim rs As Object = CreateObject("ADODB.Recordset")
        rs.ActiveConnection = cn
        rs.CursorLocation = 3
        rs.Locktype = 3
        rs.Source = "Select * from [Products.csv]"
        rs.Open()

        Dim dt As New System.Data.DataTable

        For x As Integer = 0 To rs.Fields.Count - 1
```

```vb
            dt.Columns.Add(rs.Fields(x).Name)
        Next

        rs.MoveFirst()

        Do While rs.EOF = False
            Dim dr As System.Data.DataRow = dt.NewRow
            For x As Integer = 0 To rs.Fields.Count - 1
                dr.Item(rs.Fields(x).Name) = rs.Fields(x).Value
            Next
            dt.Rows.Add(dr)
            rs.MoveNext()
        Loop

        DataGridView1.DataSource = dt

    End Sub

End Class
```

This results in:

ProductID	ProductName	SupplierID	CategoryID	QuantityPerUnit	UnitPrice	UnitsInStock	UnitsOnOrder	ReorderLevel	Discontinued
1	Chai	1	1	10 boxes x 20 bags	18	39	0	10	False
2	Chang	1	1	24 - 12 oz bottles	19	17	40	25	False
3	Aniseed Syrup	1	2	12 - 550 ml bottles	10	13	70	25	False
4	Chef Anton's Cajun Seasoning	2	2	48 - 6 oz jars	22	53	0	0	False
5	Chef Anton's Gumbo Mix	2	2	36 boxes	21.35	0	0	0	True
6	Grandma's Boysenberry Spread	3	2	12 - 8 oz jars	25	120	0	25	False
7	Uncle Bob's Organic Dried Pears	3	7	12 - 1 lb pkgs.	30	15	0	10	False
8	Northwoods Cranberry Sauce	3	2	12 - 12 oz jars	40	6	0	0	False
9	Mishi Kobe Niku	4	6	18 - 500 g pkgs.	97	29	0	0	True
10	Ikura	4	8	12 - 200 ml jars	31	31	0	0	False
11	Queso Cabrales	5	4	1 kg pkg.	21	22	30	30	False
12	Queso Manchego La Pastora	5	4	10 - 500 g pkgs.	38	86	0	0	False
13	Konbu	6	8	2 kg box	6	24	0	5	False

VB.Net does ADO and a DataView

When all else fails, run!

Below, is an example of using ADO and a DataView.

```vbnet
Public Class Form1

    Private Sub Form1_Load(sender As System.Object, e As
System.EventArgs) Handles MyBase.Load
        Dim cn As Object = CreateObject("ADODB.Connection")
        cn.Provider = "Microsoft.Jet.OleDb.4.0"
        cn.Properties("Extended Properties").Value = "text;
hdr=yes;"
        cn.Properties("Data Source").Value = "C:\"
        cn.Open()

        Dim rs As Object = CreateObject("ADODB.Recordset")
        rs.ActiveConnection = cn
        rs.CursorLocation = 3
        rs.Locktype = 3
        rs.Source = "Select * from [Products.csv]"
        rs.Open()

        Dim dt As New System.Data.DataTable

        For x As Integer = 0 To rs.Fields.Count - 1
```

```vb
            dt.Columns.Add(rs.Fields(x).Name)
        Next

        rs.MoveFirst()

        Do While rs.EOF = False
            Dim dr As System.Data.DataRow = dt.NewRow
            For x As Integer = 0 To rs.Fields.Count - 1
                dr.Item(rs.Fields(x).Name) = rs.Fields(x).Value
            Next
            dt.Rows.Add(dr)
            rs.MoveNext()
        Loop
        Dim dv As System.Data.DataView = dt.DefaultView
        DataGridView1.DataSource = dv

    End Sub

End Class
```

This results in:

ProductID	ProductName	SupplierID	CategoryID	QuantityPerUnit	UnitPrice	UnitsInStock	UnitsOnOrder	ReorderLevel	Discontinued
1	Chai	1	1	10 boxes x 20 bags	18	39	0	10	False
2	Chang	1	1	24 - 12 oz bottles	19	17	40	25	False
3	Aniseed Syrup	1	2	12 - 550 ml bottles	10	13	70	25	False
4	Chef Anton's Cajun Seasoning	2	2	48 - 6 oz jars	22	53	0	0	False
5	Chef Anton's Gumbo Mix	2	2	36 boxes	21.35	0	0	0	True
6	Grandma's Boysenberry Spread	3	2	12 - 8 oz jars	25	120	0	25	False
7	Uncle Bob's Organic Dried Pears	3	7	12 - 1 lb pkgs	30	15	0	10	False
8	Northwoods Cranberry Sauce	3	2	12 - 12 oz jars	40	6	0	0	False
9	Mishi Kobe Niku	4	6	18 - 500 g pkgs.	97	29	0	0	True
10	Ikura	4	8	12 - 200 ml jars	31	31	0	0	False
11	Queso Cabrales	5	4	1 kg pkg.	21	22	30	30	False
12	Queso Manchego La Pastora	5	4	10 - 500 g pkgs.	38	86	0	0	False
13	Konbu	6	8	2 kg box	6	24	0	5	False

VB.Net does ADO and OLEDB

This one is built in

The System.Data.OleDb.OleDbDataAdapter is capable of combining an ADO recordset with a DataSet, DataTable, or DataView. So, this begs, if I knew this from the beginning, why did I do the previous three examples for you?

The answer lies with two important facts. One, the ADO Recordset has to be in a specific format for the OleDb Provider to accept it. Two, you have more control over the manually driven routines than you do with the automation version.

```
Dim cn As Object = CreateObject("ADODB.Connection")
cn.Provider = "Microsoft.Jet.OleDb.4.0"
cn.Properties("Extended Properties").Value = "text;
hdr=yes;"
cn.Properties("Data Source").Value = "C:\"
cn.Open()

Dim rs As Object = CreateObject("ADODB.Recordset")
rs.ActiveConnection = cn
rs.CursorLocation = 3
rs.Locktype = 3
rs.Source = "Select * from [Products.csv]"
rs.Open()

Dim da As New System.Data.OleDb.OleDbDataAdapter
Dim dt As New System.Data.DataTable
da.Fill(dt, rs)

DataGridView1.DataSource = dt
```

And the results:

ProductID	ProductName	SupplierID	CategoryID	QuantityPerUnit	UnitPrice
1	Chai	1	1	10 boxes x 20 bags	18
2	Chang	1	1	24 - 12 oz bottles	19
3	Aniseed Syrup	1	2	12 - 550 ml bottles	10
4	Chef Anton's Cajun Seasoning	2	2	48 - 6 oz jars	22
5	Chef Anton's Gumbo Mix	2	2	36 boxes	21.35
6	Grandma's Boysenberry Spread	3	2	12 - 8 oz jars	25
7	Uncle Bob's Organic Dried Pears	3	7	12 - 1 lb pkgs.	30
8	Northwoods Cranberry Sauce	3	2	12 - 12 oz jars	40
9	Mishi Kobe Niku	4	6	18 - 500 g pkgs.	97
10	Ikura	4	8	12 - 200 ml jars	31
11	Queso Cabrales	5	4	1 kg pkg.	21
12	Queso Manchego La Pastora	5	4	10 - 500 g pkgs.	38
13	Konbu	6	8	2 kg box	6
14	Tofu	6	7	40 - 100 g pkgs.	23.25
15	Genen Shouyu	6	2	24 - 250 ml bottles	15.5
16	Pavlova	7	3	32 - 500 g boxes	17.45
17	Alice Mutton	7	6	20 - 1 kg tins	39
18	Camarvon Tigers	7	8	16 kg pkg.	62.5
19	Teatime Chocolate Biscuits	8	3	10 boxes x 12 pieces	9.2
20	Sir Rodney's Marmalade	8	3	30 gift boxes	81

VB.Net does ADO and Schema XML

You can even use ISAMS

You can also convert ADO – yes, even the ISAMS – to Schema XML:

```
Dim cn As Object = CreateObject("ADODB.Connection")
cn.Provider = "Microsoft.Jet.OleDb.4.0"
cn.Properties("Extended Properties").Value = "text;
hdr=yes;"
cn.Properties("Data Source").Value = "C:\"
cn.Open()

Dim rs As Object = CreateObject("ADODB.Recordset")
rs.ActiveConnection = cn
rs.CursorLocation = 3
rs.Locktype = 3
rs.Source = "Select * from [Products.csv]"
rs.Open()
rs.Save("C:\Products.xml", 1)
```

The results:

```xml
-<xml>
  -<s:Schema id="RowsetSchema">
    +<s:ElementType name="row" content="eltOnly" rs:updatable="true"></s:ElementType>
  </s:Schema>
  -<rs:data>
    <z:row ProductID="1" ProductName="Chai" SupplierID="1" CategoryID="1"
    QuantityPerUnit="10 boxes x 20 bags" UnitPrice="18" UnitsInStock="39" UnitsOnOrder="0"
    ReorderLevel="10" Discontinued="False"/>
```

VB.Net does ADOX

When Microsoft tried to kill DAO and failed

When SSD drives came along the old workhorse, DAO has come back with a vengeance. Still, ADOX is a viable way of creating an ADO Database and creating a table.

```
Dim dbPath As String
Dim dbName As String
Dim conn As Object
Const adInteger As Integer = 3
Const adKeyPrimary As Integer = 1
Const adLongVarWChar As Integer = 203
Dim ws As Object = CreateObject("WScript.Shell")

'Okay, see if the db exists
Dim fso As Object = CreateObject("Scripting.FileSystemObject")
If (fso.FileExists(fPath & "\" & dbName) = True) Then
    fso.DeleteFile()
End If

Dim oCat As Object = CreateObject("ADOX.Catalog")
oCat.Create("Provider=Microsoft.Jet.OLEDB.4.0;Data Source=" & fPath & "\"
& dbName)

Dim oTable As Object = CreateObject("ADOX.Table")
'Create the table
oTable.Name = Classname
```

```
Dim objs As Object = GetObject("Winmgmts:\.").InstancesOf(Classname)
For Each mo As ManagementObject In moc
    For Each prop As PropertyData In mo.Properties
        oTable.Columns.Append(prop.Name, adLongVarWChar)
    Next

    Exit For
Next

'Append the newly created table to the Tables Collection
oCat.Tables.Append(oTable)

oTable = Nothing
oCat = Nothing

' Open a connection.
cn = CreateObject("Adodb.Connection")
cn.ConnectionString = "Provider=Microsoft.Jet.OLEDB.4.0;" & _
    "Data Source=" & fPath & "\" & dbName & ";" & _
    "Persist Security Info=False"
cn.Open()

Dim v As Integer = 0
Dim mystr As String = ""
' Create the Employees table.


mystr = ""

objs = GetObject("Winmgmts:\.").InstancesOf(Classname)

Dim newQuery As String = "Insert Into " & Classname & " VALUES ("
For Each obj In objs
    For Each prop As Object In mo.Properties
        If mystr <> "" Then
            mystr = mystr & ", "
        End If
        mystr = mystr & "'" & GetManagementValue(prop.Name, mo) & "'"
    Next
```

```
        mystr = newQuery & mystr & ")"
        conn.Execute(mystr)
        mystr = ""
    Next

        Return "Provider=Microsoft.Jet.OLEDB.4.0;Data  Source=" & fPath & "\" &
dbName
```

VB.Net Does Arrays

The tale of two types

Normally, I would simply do one type of an array – the classical type that looks like this:

```
Dim names() as string = nothing
Dim values() as String = Nothing

ReDim Names(rs.Fields.Count)
ReDim Values(rs.RecordCount, rs.Fields.Count)
```

But it isn't the only one anymore:

```
Dim Names  As Array = Array.CreateInstance(getType(String), rs.Fields.Count)
Dim Values as Array = Array.CreateInstance(getType(String), rs.RecordCount, rs.Fields.Count)
```

VB.Net does Attribute XML

When one is not enough

This is going to sound like a broken record. There are two ways of doing Attribute XML. You can use the XmlDocument or you can just simply write out the attributes by hand.

Using the XmlDocument

```
Dim xmldoc As XmlDocument = New XmlDocument()
Dim pi As Object = xmldoc.CreateProcessingInstruction("xml",
"version='1.0' encoding='ISO-8859-1'")
Dim oRoot As Object = xmldoc.CreateElement("data")

xmldoc.AppendChild(pi)

While mocEnum.MoveNext()

    Dim mo As ManagementObject = mocEnum.Current

    Dim oNode As XmlNode = xmldoc.CreateNode(XmlNodeType.Element,
Classname, "")

    For Each prop As PropertyData In mo.Properties
```

```
            Dim oNode1 As XmlNode = xmldoc.CreateNode(XmlNodeType.Element,
"Property", "")
            Dim oAtt As XmlAttribute = xmldoc.CreateAttribute("NAME")
            oAtt.InnerText = prop.Name
            oNode1.Attributes.SetNamedItem(oAtt)

            oAtt = xmldoc.CreateAttribute("DATATYPE")
            oAtt.InnerText = prop.Qualifiers("CIMType").Value
            oNode1.Attributes.SetNamedItem(oAtt)

            oAtt = xmldoc.CreateAttribute("SIZE")
            oAtt.InnerText = Len(GetManagementValue(prop.Name, mo))
            oNode1.Attributes.SetNamedItem(oAtt)

            oAtt = xmldoc.CreateAttribute("Value")
            oAtt.InnerText = GetManagementValue(prop.Name, mo)
            oNode1.Attributes.SetNamedItem(oAtt)

            oNode.AppendChild(oNode1)

        Next

        oRoot.AppendChild(oNode)

    End While

    xmldoc.AppendChild(oRoot)
    xmldoc.Save(ws.CurrentDirectory & "\" & Classname & "_Attribute.xml")
```

The Text file

```
Dim tempstr
Dim Name
Dim Value
Dim v

Set l = CreateObject("WbemScripting.SWbemLocator")
Set svc = l.ConnectServer(".", "root\cimv2")
svc.Security_.AuthenticationLevel = 6
```

```
svc.Security_.ImpersonationLevel = 3
Set objs = svc.InstancesOf("Win32_Process")

Set ws = CreateObject("WScript.Shell")
Set fso = CreateObject("Scripting.FileSystemObject")

Set txtstream = fso.OpenTextFile("C:\Win32_Process.xml", 2, True, -2)
txtstream.WriteLine("<?xml version='1.0' encoding='iso-8859-1'?>")
txtstream.WriteLine("<data>")

For Each obj in objs
    txtstream.WriteLine("<win32_process>")
    For Each prop in obj.Properties_
        txtstream.WriteLine("<property name = """ + prop.Name + """ datatype=""" + prop.CIMType +
""" controltype = ""Textbox""" value=""" +  GetValue(prop.Name, obj) + """/>")
    Next
    txtstream.WriteLine("</win32_process>")
Next
txtstream.WriteLine("</data>")
txtstream.Close

function GetValue(ByVal Name, ByVal obj)

  Dim tempstr, pos, pName
  pName = Name
  tempstr = obj.GetObjectText_
  Name = Name + " = "
  pos = InStr(tempstr, Name)
  If pos Then

                    pos = pos + Len(Name)
                    tempstr = Mid(tempstr, pos, Len(tempstr))
                    pos = InStr(tempstr, ";")
                    tempstr = Mid(tempstr, 1, pos - 1)
                    tempstr = Replace(tempstr, Chr(34), "")
                    tempstr = Replace(tempstr, "{", "")
                    tempstr = Replace(tempstr, "}", "")
                    tempstr = Trim(tempstr)

                    If obj.Properties_(pName).CIMType = 101 Then

                        tempstr = Mid(tempstr, 5, 2) + "/" + _
                            Mid(tempstr, 7, 2) + "/" + _
                            Mid(tempstr, 1, 4) + " " + _
                            Mid(tempstr, 9, 2) + ":" + _
```

```
                    Mid(tempstr, 11, 2) + ":" + _
                    Mid(tempstr, 13, 2)

        End If

        GetValue = tempstr

    Else

        GetValue = ""

    End If

End Function
```

VB.Net does CSV files
To CSV or not to CSV

```
Dim ws As Object = CreateObject("WScript.Shell")
Dim Filename As String = ws.CurrentDirectory & "\" & Classname & ".csv"
Dim fso As Object = CreateObject("Scripting.FileSystemObject")
Dim txtstream As Object = fso.OpenTextFile(Filename, 2, True, -2)
Dim mystr As String = ""


Single Line Horizontal

   For Each mo As ManagementObject In moc
     For Each prop As PropertyData In mo.Properties

       If mystr <> "" Then
         mystr = mystr & ","
       End If

       mystr = mystr & prop.Name
     Next
     Exit For
   Next
   txtstream.WriteLine(mystr)
   mystr = ""

   For Each mo As ManagementObject In moc
     For Each prop As PropertyData In mo.Properties
```

```vb
            If mystr <> "" Then
               mystr = mystr & ","
            End If
            mystr = mystr & Chr(34) & GetManagementValue(prop.Name, mo) &
Chr(34)
         Next
         txtstream.WriteLine(mystr)
         mystr = ""
         Exit For
      Next

      txtstream.Close()
      txtstream = Nothing
      fso = Nothing
```

Multi Line Horizontal

```vb
      For Each mo As ManagementObject In moc
         For Each prop As PropertyData In mo.Properties

            If mystr <> "" Then
               mystr = mystr & ","
            End If

            mystr = mystr & prop.Name
         Next
         Exit For
      Next
      txtstream.WriteLine(mystr)
      mystr = ""

      For Each mo As ManagementObject In moc
         For Each prop As PropertyData In mo.Properties
            If mystr <> "" Then
               mystr = mystr & ","
            End If
            mystr = mystr & Chr(34) & GetManagementValue(prop.Name, mo) &
Chr(34)
         Next
         txtstream.WriteLine(mystr)
```

```
        mystr = ""
        Exit For
    Next

    txtstream.Close()
    txtstream = Nothing
    fso = Nothing
```

Single Line Vertical

```
    For Each mo As ManagementObject In moc
        For Each prop As PropertyData In mo.Properties
            txtstream.WriteLine(prop.Name        &        ","        &        Chr(34)        &
GetManagementValue(prop.Name, mo) & Chr(34))
        Next
        Exit For
    Next
    txtstream.Close()
    txtstream = Nothing
    fso = Nothing
```

Multi Line Vertical

```
    For Each prop As PropertyData In mo.Properties
        mystr = prop.Name
        For Each mo As ManagementObject In moc
            mystr = mystr & "," & Chr(34) & GetManagementValue(prop.Name, mo) &
Chr(34)
        Next
        txtstream.WriteLine(mystr)
        mystr = ""
    Next
    txtstream.Close()
    txtstream = Nothing
    fso = Nothing
```

VB.Net does DAO
The Godfather of data processing

When I came to work for Microsoft in 1996, the only way to communicate with any database that was currently being used with Microsoft Windows Products was Data Access Object or DAO for short.

DAO could connect to local or remote machines and was – still is – one of the most powerful and impressive means through which one could work with data.

The reason why Active-X Data Objects(ADO) was created because it used memory instead of physical drive space DAO was well known for using. Making it slower with respect to drive verses memory.

Well, today, the speed of USB hard drives and SSD Drives makes the speed differences between memory and physical drives a mute-point.

But there was also another reason why DAO was put on the back burner.

SQL Server.

It isn't hard to imagine why. DAO connecting to a remote machine where the database was located works much like SQL Server clients can connect to a remote version of SQL Server. But DAO wasn't and still isn't limited to just SQL Server.

It can connect to all different kinds of databases such as Indexed Sequential Access Method or ISAM and Open Database Connectivity (ODBC) drivers can be used as well.

While it is true that ADO can do the same, A lot of what ADO uses and, for certain, what the .Net Framework uses has been built on top of DAO and ODBC advanced programmer's interfaces (APIs). Which is why specific types of Namespaces: ADO, ODBC, OLEDB, and SQL Client exists as separate ways to connect to different database types.

How To connect to DAO

Connecting to DAO is as simple as this:

Using DAO.DBEngine.35:

```
Dim DBEngine As Object = CreateObject("DAO.DBEngine.35")
Dim DB As Object = DBEngine.OpenDatabase("C:\NWIND.MDB")
```

Using DAO.DBEngine.36:

```
Dim DBEngine As Object = CreateObject("DAO.DBEngine.36")
Dim DB As Object = DBEngine.OpenDatabase("C:\NWIND.MDB")
```

Using DAO.DBEngine.120:

```
Dim DBEngine As Object = CreateObject("DAO.DBEngine.120")
Dim DB As Object = DBEngine.OpenDatabase("C:\NWIND.MDB")
```

Of Course, you could create a Workspace and make the code much more complex but if you just want to get the job done, the above code gets the job done.

ISAMS

Did you know you can use a wide variety of text files as databases?

It's true, In fact, if you have a table inside a webpage, using the right ISAM or ODBC Driver, you can connect to it and glean from it the table information and convert it into a different type of database format.

In plain English, it is a text file. The idea was to take a folder and call it a database and then take a file and call it a table. Similar to the way JSOM works.

One of the biggest issues – and one that brought smiles to our technical support faces – was to explain, politely to our customers that the reason why they were getting an error when they tried to create a database was the fact that the folder already existed.

Every text file you create will have some kind of delimiter. Otherwise, placing information into a text file would be just another text file and you couldn't reuse the information because there would be nothing a program – including ours – could use to separate one field from another.

These are all various files we're going to be covering, so they really don't change that much. But they are used quite often as data storage and data files.

Of course, CSV or coma delimited is just one of dozens of possibilities. And all of these are fairly easy to code. You enumerate through tstr and Tstr and then add the delimiter of choice to separate the fields.

Problem is, it doesn't work. At least, not yet. It will soon. In fact, after I get done with it, you are going to become a master of Delimited files.

ISAMS USED WITH DAO.DBEngine.35

ISAM Engine	Is The Folder Path The Database	Is The File Name The Database	Are Tables Internal
dBase 5.0	Yes	No	No
dBase III	Yes	No	No
dBase IV	Yes	No	No
Excel 3.0	No	Yes	Yes
Excel 4.0	No	Yes	Yes
Excel 5.0	No	Yes	Yes
Excel 6.0	No	Yes	Yes
FoxPro 2.0	Yes	No	No
FoxPro 2.5	Yes	No	No
FoxPro 2.6	Yes	No	No
FoxPro 3.0	Yes	No	No
HTML Export	No	Yes	Yes
HTML Import	No	Yes	Yes
Jet 2.x	No	Yes	Yes
Lotus WK1	Yes	No	No
Lotus WK3	Yes	No	No
Lotus WK4	Yes	No	No
Paradox 3.X	Yes	No	No
Paradox 4.X	Yes	No	No
Paradox 5.X	Yes	No	No
Text	No	No	No

```
Dim DBEngine As Object = CreateObject("DAO.DBEngine.35")
```

dBase III, DBASE IV, DBASE 5.0

Dim DB As Object = DBEngine.OpenDatabase("C:\dBase Folder", false, false, "dBase III; hdr=yes;")
Or:
Dim DB As Object = DBEngine.OpenDatabase("C:\dBase Folder", false, false, "dBase IV; hdr=yes;")
Or:
Dim DB As Object = DBEngine.OpenDatabase("C:\dBase Folder", false, false, "dBase 5.0; hdr=yes;")

Excel 3.0, Excel 4.0; EXCEL 5.0, excel 6.0

Dim DB As Object = DBEngine.OpenDatabase("C:\Excel Files\Filename", false, false, "Excel 3.0; hdr=yes;")
Or:
Dim DB As Object = DBEngine.OpenDatabase("C:\Excel Files\Filename", false, false, "Excel 4.0; hdr=yes;")
Or:
Dim DB As Object = DBEngine.OpenDatabase("C:\Excel Files\Filename", false, false, "Excel 5.0; hdr=yes;")
Or:
Dim DB As Object = DBEngine.OpenDatabase("C:\Excel Files\Filename", false, false, "Excel 6.0; hdr=yes;")

FOX Pro 2.0, Fox Pro 2.5, Fox Pro 2.6, Fox Pro 3.0

Dim DB As Object = DBEngine.OpenDatabase("C:\FoxPro Folder", false, false, "Fox Pro 2.0; hdr=yes;")
Or:
Dim DB As Object = DBEngine.OpenDatabase("C:\FoxPro Folder", false, false, "Fox Pro 2.4; hdr=yes;")
Or:
Dim DB As Object = DBEngine.OpenDatabase("C:\FoxPro Folder", false, false, "Fox Pro 2.5; hdr=yes;")
Or:
Dim DB As Object = DBEngine.OpenDatabase("C:\FoxPro Folder", false, false, "Fox Pro 3.0; hdr=yes;")

HTML IMPORT

```
Dim DB As Object = DBEngine.OpenDatabase("C:\HTML Files\Filename", false, false, "HTML Import; hdr=yes;" )
```
Jet 2.x

```
Dim DB As Object = DBEngine.OpenDatabase("C:\Access\Filename", false, false, "Jet 2.x; hdr=yes;" )
```
Or:
```
Dim DB As Object =DBEngine.OpenDatabase("C:\Access\Filename", false, false, "Jet 3.x; hdr=yes;" )
```

LOTUS WK1, LOTUS WK3, Lotus Wk4

```
Dim DB As Object = DBEngine.OpenDatabase("C:\Lotus\Filename", false, false, "Lotus WK1; hdr=yes;" )
```
Or:
```
Dim DB As Object = DBEngine.OpenDatabase("C:\Lotus\Filename", false, false, "Lotus WK3; hdr=yes;" )
```
Or:
```
Dim DB As Object = DBEngine.OpenDatabase("C:\Lotus\Filename", false, false, "Lotus WK4; hdr=yes;" )
```
Paradox 3.X, PARADOX 4.x, PARADOX 5.x

```
Dim DB As Object = DBEngine.OpenDatabase("C:\Paradox Folder", false, false, "Paradox 3.X; hdr=yes;" )
```
Or:
```
Dim DB As Object = DBEngine.OpenDatabase("C:\Paradox Folder", false, false, "Paradox 4.X; hdr=yes;" )
```
Or:
```
Dim DB As Object = DBEngine.OpenDatabase("C:\Paradox Folder", false, false, "Paradox 5.X; hdr=yes;" )
```
Text

```
Dim DB As Object = DBEngine.OpenDatabase("C:\Text Folder", false, false, "TEXT; hdr=yes; Format=CSVDelimited;" )
```

ISAMS USED WITH DAO.DBEngine.36

ISAM Engine	Is The Folder The Database	Is The File Name The Database	Are Tables Internal
dBase 5.0	Yes	No	No
dBase III	Yes	No	No
dBase IV	Yes	No	No
Excel 3.0	No	Yes	Yes
Excel 4.0	No	Yes	Yes
Excel 5.0	No	Yes	Yes
Excel 8.0	No	Yes	Yes
HTML Export	No	Yes	Yes
HTML Import	No	Yes	Yes
Jet 2.x	No	Yes	Yes
Lotus WJ2	Yes	No	No
Lotus WJ3	Yes	No	No
Lotus WK1	Yes	No	No
Lotus WK3	Yes	No	No
Lotus WK4	Yes	No	No
Paradox 3.X	Yes	No	No
Paradox 4.X	Yes	No	No
Paradox 5.X	Yes	No	No
Text	No	No	No

Below is a function that connects to the various ISAMS.

```
Dim DBEngine As Object = CreateObject("DAO.DBEngine.36")
Dim DB As Object = DBEngine.OpenDatabase("C:\NWIND.MDB")
```

dBase III, DBASE IV, DBASE 5.0

```
Dim DB As Object = DBEngine.OpenDatabase("C:\dBase Folder", false, false,
"dBase III; hdr=yes;" )
    Or:
    Dim DB As Object = DBEngine.OpenDatabase("C:\dBase Folder", false, false,
"dBase IV; hdr=yes;" )
    Or:
    Dim DB As Object = DBEngine.OpenDatabase("C:\dBase Folder", false, false,
"dBase 5.0; hdr=yes;" )
```

Excel 3.0, Excel 4.0; EXCEL 5.0, excel 8.0

```
Dim DB As Object = DBEngine.OpenDatabase("C:\Excel Files\Filename", false,
false, "Excel 3.0; hdr=yes;" )
    Or:
    Dim DB As Object = DBEngine.OpenDatabase("C:\Excel Files\Filename", false,
false, "Excel 4.0; hdr=yes;" )
    Or:
    Dim DB As Object = DBEngine.OpenDatabase("C:\Excel Files\Filename", false,
false, "Excel 5.0; hdr=yes;" )
    Or:
    Dim DB As Object = DBEngine.OpenDatabase("C:\Excel Files\Filename", false,
false, "Excel 8.0; hdr=yes;" )
```

HTML IMPORT

```
Dim DB As Object = DBEngine.OpenDatabase("C:\HTML Files\Filename", false,
false, "HTML Import; hdr=yes;" )
```

Jet 2.x, jet 3.x

```
Dim DB As Object = DBEngine.OpenDatabase("C:\Access\Filename", false, false,
"Jet 2.x; hdr=yes;" )
    Or:
    Dim DB As Object =DBEngine.OpenDatabase("C:\Access\Filename", false, false,
"Jet 3.x; hdr=yes;" )
```

Lotus WJ2, Lotus WJ3

```
Dim DB As Object = DBEngine.OpenDatabase("C:\Lotus\Filename", false, false,
"Lotus WJ2; hdr=yes;" )
    Or:
Dim DB As Object = DBEngine.OpenDatabase("C:\Lotus\Filename", false, false,
"Lotus WJ3; hdr=yes;" )
```

LOTUS WK1, LOTUS WK3, LOTUS WK4

```
Dim DB As Object = DBEngine.OpenDatabase("C:\Lotus\Filename", false, false,
"Lotus WK1; hdr=yes;" )
    Or:
Dim DB As Object = DBEngine.OpenDatabase("C:\Lotus\Filename", false, false,
"Lotus WK3; hdr=yes;" )
    Or:
Dim DB As Object = DBEngine.OpenDatabase("C:\Lotus\Filename", false, false,
"Lotus WK4; hdr=yes;" )
```

Paradox 3.X, PARADOX 4.x, PARADOX 5.x, Paradox 7.x

```
Dim DB As Object = DBEngine.OpenDatabase("C:\Paradox Folder", false, false,
"Paradox 3.X; hdr=yes;" )
    Or:
Dim DB As Object = DBEngine.OpenDatabase("C:\Paradox Folder", false, false,
"Paradox 4.X; hdr=yes;" )
    Or:
Dim DB As Object = DBEngine.OpenDatabase("C:\Paradox Folder", false, false,
"Paradox 5.X; hdr=yes;" )
Dim DB As Object = DBEngine.OpenDatabase("C:\Paradox Folder", false, false,
"Paradox 7.X; hdr=yes;" )
```

Text

```
Dim DB As Object = DBEngine.OpenDatabase("C:\Text Folder", false, false,
"TEXT; hdr=yes; Format=CSVDelimited;" )
```

VB.Net working with DAO and Access

Never a dull moment

This is an oxymoron because ACCESS depends on do much of the heavy lifting. With that said, let's take a look at the way DAO creates an Access Database and then take a look at the way Access does it.

The different versions of Access are the following:

```
dbVersion10 =      1
dbVersion11 =      8
dbVersion20 =     16
dbVersion30 =     32
dbVersion40 =     64
dbVersion120 =   128
```

Encryption:

```
dbEncrypt =      2
dbDecrypt =      4
```

Languages:

```
dbSortNeutral = 0x0400;
dbSortArabic = 0x0401;
dbSortCyrillic = 0x0419;
dbSortCzech = 0x0405;
dbSortDutch = 0x0413;
```

```
dbSortGeneral = 0x0409;
dbSortGreek = 0x0408;
dbSortHebrew = 0x040D;
dbSortHungarian = 0x040E;
dbSortIcelandic = 0x040F;
dbSortNorwdan = 0x0406;
dbSortPDXIntl = 0x0409;
dbSortPDXNor = 0x0406;
dbSortPDXSwe = 0x041D;
dbSortPolish = 0x0415;
dbSortSpanish = 0x040A;
dbSortSwedFin = 0x041D;
dbSortTurkish = 0x041F;
dbSortJapanese = 0x0411;
dbSortChineseSimplified = 0x0804;
dbSortChineseTraditional = 0x0404;
dbSortKorean = 0x0412;
dbSortThai = 0x041E;
dbSortSlovenian = 0x0424;
dbSortUndefined = 0x0FFF;
```

Below are some examples of using create a database:

```
Const dbLangGeneral = ";LANGID=0x0409;CP=1252;COUNTRY=0"
Dim DBEngine As Object = CreateObject("DAO.DBEngine.120")
Dim    DB    As    Object    =    dbEngine.CreateDatabase("C:\MyFirst.accdb",
dbLangGeneral, dbVersion120)

Dim DBEngine As Object = CreateObject("DAO.DBEngine.36")
Dim    DB    As    Object    =    dbEngine.CreateDatabase("C:\MyFirst.accdb",
dbLangGeneral, dbVersion40)

Dim DBEngine As Object = CreateObject("DAO.DBEngine.35")
Dim DB As Object = dbEngine.CreateDatabase("C:\MyFirst.mdb", dbLangGeneral,
dbVersion30)
```

The four ways you can create an Access Database through automation:

```
Dim oAccess As Object = CreateObject("Access.Application")
oAccess.Visible = true
```

```
oAccess.NewCurrentDatabase("C:\test\Myfirst.mdb", 9)

Dim oAccess As Object = CreateObject("Access.Application")
oAccess.Visible = true
oAccess.NewCurrentDatabase("C:\test\Myfirst.mdb", 10)

Dim oAccess As Object = CreateObject("Access.Application")
oAccess.Visible = true
oAccess.NewCurrentDatabase("C:\test\Myfirst.accdb", 12)

Dim oAccess As Object = CreateObject("Access.Application")
oAccess.Visible = true
oAccess.NewCurrentDatabase("C:\test\Myfirst.accdb", 0)
```

Below, are two ways of opening an Access database:

```
Dim oAccess As Object = CreateObject("Access.Application")
oAccess.Visible = true
  oAccess.OpenCurrentDatabase("C:\test\Myfirst.mdb")

Dim oAccess As Object = CreateObject("Access.Application")
oAccess.Visible = true
  oAccess.OpenCurrentDatabase ("C:\test\Myfirst.accdb")
```

All well and good, but if you don't know the database, how in the heck can you know what the names of the tables are?

Well, that's where this code saves the day:

```
Dim DBEngine As Object = CreateObject("DAO.DBEngine.36")
Dim DB As Object = DBEngine.OpenDatabase("C:\NWIND.MDB")

Dim tbldef As Object = db. TableDefs
for each tbl in tbldefs
   WScript.Echo("Name = " & tbl.Properties("Name").Value)
   WScript.Echo("RecordCount = " & tbl.Properties("RecordCount").Value)
   WScript.Echo(" ")
next
```

Name	RecordCount

Categories	8
Customers	91
Employees	9
Order Details	2155
Orders	830
Products	77
Shippers	3
Suppliers	29

Okay, so what about Queries?

Alphabetical List of Products	Order Details Extended	Sales by Category
Catalog	Order Subtotals	Sales by Year
Category Sales for 1995	Orders Wry	Sales Totals by Amount
Current Product List	Product Sales for 1995	Summary of Sales by Quarter
Customers and Suppliers by City	Products Above Average Price	Summary of Sales by Year
Employee Sales by Country	Products by Category	Ten Most Expensive Products
Invoices	Quarterly Orders	
Invoices Filter	Quarterly Orders by Product	

The details for Name Alphabetical List of Products QueryDef are below:

Name Alphabetical List of Products
DateCreated 6/21/1996 6:18:31 PM
LastUpdated 9/23/1996 3:23:36 PM
Type 0
SQL SELECT DISTINCTROW Products.*, Categories.CategoryName
FROM Categories INNER JOIN Products ON Categories.CategoryID = Products.CategoryID
WHERE (((Products.Discontinued)=No));
Updatable True
Connect
ReturnsRecords True

58

ODBCTimeout 0
RecordsAffected 0
MaxRecords 0
RecordLocks 0
OrderByOn False
Description Underlying query for Alphabetical List of Products report.

Now that we are armed and dangerous, I want to mention something here that most forget to mention. When you create a query string, use [ ] brackets around the table name. While it is not necessary around tables like Products, it is required if there are spaces in the table name. So, it just makes sense, since it doesn't have an effect on your query with table names that don't have brackets to do it with all table names.

Make it a habit. The first time you forget, and your query fails, you're going to wish you had.

With that said, let's get down to business.

VB.Net does DAO and the Dataset

Always this easy

Name a bound control in VB.Net and if you want to bind your data to it, the Dataset, DataReader, Datatable and Dataview. Technically, the Dataset is a collection of Datatables and the Dataview is the default view of the Datatable. So, you really only have two: The Datatable and the DataReader.

```
        Dim DBEngine As Object = CreateObject("DAO.DBEngine.36")
        Dim db As Object = DBEngine.OpenDataBase("", False,
False, "text; hdr=yes;Database=C:\")
        Dim rs As Object = db.OpenRecordset("Select * from
[Products.csv]")

        Dim ds As New System.Data.DataSet
        Dim dt As New System.Data.DataTable
        ds.Tables.Add(dt)

        For x As Integer = 0 To rs.Fields.Count - 1
            ds.Tables(0).Columns.Add(rs.Fields(x).Name)
        Next

        rs.MoveFirst()
        Do While rs.EOF = False
            Dim dr As System.Data.DataRow = ds.Tables(0).NewRow
            For x As Integer = 0 To rs.Fields.Count - 1
                dr.Item(rs.Fields(x).Name) = rs.Fields(x).Value
            Next
            ds.Tables(0).Rows.Add(dr)
```

```
        rs.MoveNext()
Loop

    DataGridView1.DataSource = ds.Tables(0)
```

The results:

ProductID	ProductName	SupplierID	CategoryID	QuantityPerUnit
1	Chai	1	1	10 boxes x 20 bags
2	Chang	1	1	24 - 12 oz bottles
3	Aniseed Syrup	1	2	12 - 550 ml bottles
4	Chef Anton's Cajun Seasoning	2	2	48 - 6 oz jars
5	Chef Anton's Gumbo Mix	2	2	36 boxes
6	Grandma's Boysenberry Spread	3	2	12 - 8 oz jars
7	Uncle Bob's Organic Dried Pears	3	7	12 - 1 lb pkgs.
8	Northwoods Cranberry Sauce	3	2	12 - 12 oz jars
9	Mishi Kobe Niku	4	6	18 - 500 g pkgs.
10	Ikura	4	8	12 - 200 ml jars
11	Queso Cabrales	5	4	1 kg pkg.
12	Queso Manchego La Pastora	5	4	10 - 500 g pkgs.
13	Konbu	6	8	2 kg box
14	Tofu	6	7	40 - 100 g pkgs.
15	Genen Shouyu	6	2	24 - 250 ml bottles
16	Pavlova	7	3	32 - 500 g boxes
17	Alice Mutton	7	6	20 - 1 kg tins
18	Carnarvon Tigers	7	8	16 kg pkg.
19	Teatime Chocolate Biscuits	8	3	10 boxes x 12 pieces
20	Sir Rodney's Marmalade	8	3	30 gift boxes
21	Sir Rodney's Scones	8	3	24 pkgs. x 4 pieces

VB.Net does DAO and Datatable

One more to go!

Here's an example of DAO populating the DataTable as the DataSource for the DataGridView:

```vbnet
Dim DBEngine As Object = CreateObject("DAO.DBEngine.36")
Dim db As Object = DBEngine.OpenDataBase("", False,
False, "text; hdr=yes;Database=C:\")
Dim rs As Object = db.OpenRecordset("Select * from
[Products.csv]")


Dim dt As New System.Data.DataTable
For x As Integer = 0 To rs.Fields.Count - 1
    dt.Columns.Add(rs.Fields(x).Name)
Next

rs.MoveFirst()
Do While rs.EOF = False
    Dim dr As System.Data.DataRow = dt.NewRow
    For x As Integer = 0 To rs.Fields.Count - 1
        dr.Item(rs.Fields(x).Name) = rs.Fields(x).Value
    Next
    ds.Tables(0).Rows.Add(dr)
    rs.MoveNext()
Loop

DataGridView1.DataSource = dt
```

The results:

ProductID	ProductName	SupplierID	CategoryID	QuantityPerUnit
1	Chai	1	1	10 boxes x 20 bags
2	Chang	1	1	24 - 12 oz bottles
3	Aniseed Syrup	1	2	12 - 550 ml bottles
4	Chef Anton's Cajun Seasoning	2	2	48 - 6 oz jars
5	Chef Anton's Gumbo Mix	2	2	36 boxes
6	Grandma's Boysenberry Spread	3	2	12 - 8 oz jars
7	Uncle Bob's Organic Dried Pears	3	7	12 - 1 lb pkgs.
8	Northwoods Cranberry Sauce	3	2	12 - 12 oz jars
9	Mishi Kobe Niku	4	6	18 - 500 g pkgs.
10	Ikura	4	8	12 - 200 ml jars
11	Queso Cabrales	5	4	1 kg pkg.
12	Queso Manchego La Pastora	5	4	10 - 500 g pkgs.
13	Konbu	6	8	2 kg box
14	Tofu	6	7	40 - 100 g pkgs.
15	Genen Shouyu	6	2	24 - 250 ml bottles
16	Pavlova	7	3	32 - 500 g boxes
17	Alice Mutton	7	6	20 - 1 kg tins
18	Camarvon Tigers	7	8	16 kg pkg.
19	Teatime Chocolate Biscuits	8	3	10 boxes x 12 pieces
20	Sir Rodney's Marmalade	8	3	30 gift boxes
21	Sir Rodney's Scones	8	3	24 pkgs. x 4 pieces

VB.Net does DAO and a DataView

Yep, it is here

Here's an example of DAO populating the DataTable and then using the DefaultView as the DataSource for the DataGridView:

```vb
Dim DBEngine As Object = CreateObject("DAO.DBEngine.36")
Dim db As Object = DBEngine.OpenDataBase("", False,
False, "text; hdr=yes;Database=C:\")
Dim rs As Object = db.OpenRecordset("Select * from
[Products.csv]")


Dim dt As New System.Data.DataTable
For x As Integer = 0 To rs.Fields.Count - 1
    dt.Columns.Add(rs.Fields(x).Name)
Next

rs.MoveFirst()
Do While rs.EOF = False
    Dim dr As System.Data.DataRow = dt.NewRow
    For x As Integer = 0 To rs.Fields.Count - 1
        dr.Item(rs.Fields(x).Name) = rs.Fields(x).Value
    Next
    ds.Tables(0).Rows.Add(dr)
    rs.MoveNext()
Loop

Dim dv As System.Data.DataView = dt.DefaultView
```

```
DataGridView1.DataSource = dv
```

The results:

ProductID	ProductName	SupplierID	CategoryID	QuantityPerUnit
1	Chai	1	1	10 boxes x 20 bags
2	Chang	1	1	24 - 12 oz bottles
3	Aniseed Syrup	1	2	12 - 550 ml bottles
4	Chef Anton's Cajun Seasoning	2	2	48 - 6 oz jars
5	Chef Anton's Gumbo Mix	2	2	36 boxes
6	Grandma's Boysenberry Spread	3	2	12 - 8 oz jars
7	Uncle Bob's Organic Dried Pears	3	7	12 - 1 lb pkgs.
8	Northwoods Cranberry Sauce	3	2	12 - 12 oz jars
9	Mishi Kobe Niku	4	6	18 - 500 g pkgs.
10	Ikura	4	8	12 - 200 ml jars
11	Queso Cabrales	5	4	1 kg pkg.
12	Queso Manchego La Pastora	5	4	10 - 500 g pkgs.
13	Konbu	6	8	2 kg box
14	Tofu	6	7	40 - 100 g pkgs.
15	Genen Shouyu	6	2	24 - 250 ml bottles
16	Pavlova	7	3	32 - 500 g boxes
17	Alice Mutton	7	6	20 - 1 kg tins
18	Camarvon Tigers	7	8	16 kg pkg.
19	Teatime Chocolate Biscuits	8	3	10 boxes x 12 pieces
20	Sir Rodney's Marmalade	8	3	30 gift boxes
21	Sir Rodney's Scones	8	3	24 pkgs. x 4 pieces

VB.Net does Dictionary Objects

Optional ways of doing things are good

As with almost everything in VB.Net, there are two – or more – ways to do almost anything. The COM way and the .NET way. Here's the old school way:

```
Dim dNames as Scripting.Dictionary = new Scripting.Dictionary
Dim dRows as Scripting.Dictionary = new Scripting.Dictionary


For x = 0 to ubound(Names) -1
   dNames.Add(x , names(x))
Next

For y = 0 to Values.GetLength(0)-1
   Dim dCols as new Scripting.Dictionary
   For x = 0 to ubound(Names) -1
     dCols.Add(x, Values(y, x))
   Next
   dt.Rows.Add(y, dCols)
Next
```

To reverse this so that we could use this later to bind to a DataSource:

```
Dim nkeys as Object = dNames.Keys
For x = 0 to ubound(nkeys) -1
   dt.Columns.Add(dNames.Item(keys(x)), dNames.Item(keys(x)))
Next
```

```
Dim rkeys as Object = dRows.Keys


For y = 0 to UBound(rkeys)-1
   Dim dr as System.Data.DataRow = dt.NewRow
   Dim dCols as Scripting.Dictionary = dRows.Item(rkeys(y))
   Dim ckeys as Object = dCols.Keys
   For x = 0 to ubound(ckeys) -1
     dr.Item(dNames.Item(nkeys(x)) = dCols.Item(ckeys(x))
   Next
   dt.Rows.Add(dr)
Next


DataGridView1.DataSource = dt
```

Now that's one way to do it. Below, is the other.

```
Dim dNames As New System.Collections.Generic.Dictionary(Of Integer, String)
Dim dRows As New System.Collections.Generic.Dictionary(Of Integer,
System.Collections.Generic.Dictionary(Of Integer, String))

For x = 0 to ubound(Names) -1
   dNames.Add(x , names(x))
Next

For y = 0 to Values.GetLength(0)-1
   Dim dNames As New System.Collections.Generic.Dictionary(Of Integer, String)
   For x = 0 to ubound(Names) -1
     dCols.Add(x, Values(y, x))
   Next
   dt.Rows.Add(y, dCols)
Next
```

Again, to reverse the process:

```
For x = 0 to dNames.Keys.Count -1
   dt.Columns.Add(dNames.Item(x), dNames.Item(x))
Next

For y = 0 To dRows.Keys.Count - 1
   Dim dr As System.Data.DataRow = dt.NewRow
```

```
        Dim dCols As System.Collections.Generic.Dictionary(Of Integer, String) =
dRows.Item(y)

    For x = 0 To dCols.Keys.Count - 1
        dr.Item(dNames.Item(x)) = dCols.Item(x)
    Next
    dt.Rows.Add(dr)
Next

DataGridView1.DataSource = dt
```

VB.Net does Element XML
The backbone of static data

```
Dim ws As Object = CreateObject("WScript.Shell")
Dim fso As Object = CreateObject("Scripting.FileSystemObject")
Dim txtstream As Object = fso.OpenTextfile(ws.CurrentDirectory & "\" &
Classname & ".xml", 2, True, -2)


txtstream.WriteLine("<?xml version=""1.0"" encoding=""iso-8859-1""?>")
txtstream.WriteLine("<data>")
Do While mocEnum.MoveNext
    txtstream.WriteLine("<" & Classname & ">")
    obj = mocEnum.Current
    For Each Prop As Object In obj.Properties
        txtstream.WriteLine("<"    &    Prop.Name    &    "><![CDATA["    &
GetValue(Prop.Name, obj) & "]]></" & Prop.Name & ">")
    Next
    txtstream.WriteLine("</" & Classname & ">")
Loop
txtstream.WriteLine("</data>")
txtstream.Close()
```

VB.Net does XML for XSL

Making xml depend on XSL for rendering

Below, is the code for creating an xml file that depends on a xsl file for rending the static data.

```
Dim ws As Object = CreateObject("WScript.Shell")
Dim fso As Object = CreateObject("Scripting.FileSystemObject")
Dim txtstream As Object = fso.OpenTextfile(ws.CurrentDirectory & "\" &
Classname & ".xml", 2, True, -2)
    txtstream.WriteLine("<?xml version=""1.0"" encoding=""iso-8859-1""?>")
    txtstream.WriteLine("<?xml-stylesheet    type=""Text/xsl""    href=""C:\"    &
classname & ".xsl""?>")
    txtstream.WriteLine("<data>")
    Do While mocEnum.MoveNext
        txtstream.WriteLine("<" & Classname & ">")
        Dim mo as ManagementObject = mocEnum.Current
        For Each Prop As PropertyData In mo.Properties
            txtstream.WriteLine("<"    &    Prop.Name    &    "><![CDATA["    &
GetValue(Prop.Name, obj) & "]]></" & Prop.Name & ">")
        Next
        txtstream.WriteLine("</" & Classname & ">")
    Loop
    txtstream.WriteLine("</data>")
    txtstream.Close()
```

VB.Net does CSV files

ISAMs aren't the only way you can create csv files

Welcome to the department of redundancy department. Below is the code for creating csv files for various purposes.

```vb
Dim ws As Object = CreateObject("WScript.Shell")
Dim Filename As String = ws.CurrentDirectory & "\" & Classname & ".csv"
Dim fso As Object = CreateObject("Scripting.FileSystemObject")
Dim txtstream As Object = fso.OpenTextFile(Filename, 2, True, -2)
Dim mystr As String = ""

For Each mo As ManagementObject In moc
    For Each prop As PropertyData In mo.Properties
        If mystr <> "" Then
            mystr = mystr & ","
        End If
        mystr = mystr & prop.Name
    Next
    Exit For
Next
txtstream.WriteLine(mystr)
mystr = ""

For Each mo As ManagementObject In moc
    For Each prop As PropertyData In mo.Properties
```

```
        If mystr <> "" Then
            mystr = mystr & ","
        End If
        mystr = mystr & Chr(34) & GetManagementValue(prop.Name, mo) & Chr(34)
    Next

    txtstream.WriteLine(mystr)
    mystr = ""
    Exit For
Next
txtstream.Close()
txtstream = Nothing
fso = Nothing

ws.Run(ws.CurrentDirectory & "\" & Classname & ".csv")
```

or you can do it this the Excel way.

Creating various set and customized text files for Excel
And it is faster than trying to automate Excel

If you want Excel to, well, excel, you should consider writing your delimited text files first and then bring them in as workbooks. Below are various text formats Excel is expecting the files to be in including customized delimiters.

```
Dim oExcel as Object = CreateObject(Excel.Application)
oExcel.Visible = true
Dim wb As Object = oExcel.Workbooks.OpenText(ws.CurrentDirectory & "\" &
Classname & ".csv")
```

The fact is, creating a text file is much faster than trying to populate the file using automation. The key is to know what the command line should look like when you want to open the file through automation. And that is where the below tables should help you set the correct variables and in the correct sequence.

Dim wb as Object

For a Tab delimited file

Values	Comments
[string]filename ="C:\Test\Excel.txt"	The name of the file you just created
[int]Origin =437	The country code. US is 437
[int]StartRow =1	Set to 1
[int]DataType – 1	1 = Delimited of 2 =FixedWidth
[int]TextQualifier = -4142	-4142 = NoStringDelimiter, 2=", 1 = '
[bool]ConsecutiveDelimiter = false	based on what I've seen, use false. Could cause issues.
[bool]Tab =true	Since this is tab, set to true
[bool]Semicolon=false	Since this is not, set to false
[bool]Comma=false	Since this is not, set to false
[bool]Space=false	Since this is not, set to false
[bool]Other=false	Since this is not, set to false
[string]OtherChar	Don't include and end your

wb = oExcel.Workbooks.OpenText("C:\Test\Excel.txt",437,1,1,2,false, true, false, false, false, false)

Semicolon Delimited

Values	Comments
[string]filename ="C:\Test\Excel.txt"	The name of the file you just created
[int]Origin =437	The country code. US is 437
[int]StartRow =1	Set to 1
[int]DataType = 1	1 = Delimited of 2 =FixedWidth
[int]TextQualifier = 2	-4142 = NoStringDelimiter, 2=", 1 = '
[bool]ConsecutiveDelimiter = false	based on what I've seen, use false. Could cause issues.
[bool]Tab =false	Since this is not, set to true

[bool]Semicolon=true	Since this is, set to false
[bool]Comma=false	Since this is not, set to false
[bool]Space=false	Since this is not, set to false
[bool]Other=false	Since this is not, set to false
[string]OtherChar	Don't include and end your

wb = oExcel.Workbooks.OpenText("C:\Test\Excel.txt",437,1,1,2,false, false, true, false, false, false)

Coma Delimited

Either just name the file with the .csv or use the .txt and:

Values	Comments
[string]filename ="C:\Test\Excel.txt"	The name of the file you just created
[int]Origin =437	The country code. US is 437
[int]StartRow =1	Set to 1
[int]DataType = 1	1 = Delimited of 2 =FixedWidth
[int]TextQualifier = 2	-4142 = NoStringDelimiter, 2=", 1 = '
[bool]ConsecutiveDelimiter = false	based on what I've seen, use false. Could cause issues.
[bool]Tab =false	Tells Excel this is not a tab delimited file
[bool]Semicolon=false	Since this is not, set to true
[bool]Comma=true	Since this is true, set to true
[bool]Space=false	Since this is not, set to false
[bool]Other=false	Since this is not, set to false
[string]OtherChar	Don't include and end your connection string

wb = oExcel.Workbooks.OpenText("C:\Test\Excel.txt",437,1,1,2,false, false, false, true, false, false)

Fixed Width

Either just name the file with the .csv or use the .txt and:

Values	Comments
[string]filename ="C:\Test\Excel.txt"	The name of the file you just created
[int]Origin =437	The country code. US is 437
[int]StartRow =1	Set to 1
[int]DataType = 2	1 = Delimited of 2 =FixedWidth
[int]TextQualifier = -4142	-4142 = NoStringDelimiter, 2=", 1 = '
[bool]ConsecutiveDelimiter = false	based on what I've seen, use false. Could cause issues.
[bool]Tab =false	Since this is not, set to true
[bool]Semicolon=false	Since this is not, set to false
[bool]Comma=false	Since this is not, set to false
[bool]Space=true	Since this is, set to false
[bool]Other=false	Since this is not, set to false
[string]OtherChar	Don't include and end your

wb = oExcel.Workbooks.OpenText("C:\Test\Excel.txt",437,1,2,-4142,false, false, false, false, true, false)

Tilde Delimited

Values	Comments
[string]filename ="C:\Test\Excel.txt"	The name of the file you just created
[int]Origin =437	The country code. US is 437
[int]StartRow =1	Set to 1
[int]DataType = 1	1 = Delimited of 2 =FixedWidth
[int]TextQualifier = 2	-4142 = NoStringDelimiter, 2=", 1 = '
[bool]ConsecutiveDelimiter = false	based on what I've seen, use

	false. Could cause issues.
[bool]Tab =false	Since this is not, set to true
[bool]Semicolon=false	Since this is not, set to false
[bool]Comma=false	Since this is not, set to false
[bool]Space=false	Since this is not, set to false
[bool]Other=false	Since this is, set to false
[string]OtherChar = "~"	Include and end your

wb = oExcel.Workbooks.OpenText("C:\Test\Excel.txt",437,1,1,2,false, false, false, false, false, true, "~")

Exclamation Delimited

Either just name the file with the .csv or use the .txt and:

Values	Comments
[string]filename ="C:\Test\Excel.txt"	The name of the file you just created
[int]Origin =437	The country code. US is 437
[int]StartRow =1	Set to 1
[int]DataType = 1	1 = Delimited of 2 =FixedWidth
[int]TextQualifier = 2	-4142 = NoStringDelimiter, 2=", 1 = '
[bool]ConsecutiveDelimiter = false	based on what I've seen, use false. Could cause issues.
[bool]Tab =false	Since this is not, set to true
[bool]Semicolon=false	Since this is not, set to false
[bool]Comma=false	Since this is not, set to false
[bool]Space=false	Since this is not, set to false
[bool]Other=true	Since this is, set to false
[string]OtherChar = "!"	Include at end your string

```
wb = oExcel.Workbooks.OpenText("C:\Test\Excel.txt",437,1,1,2,false, false, false,
false, false, true, "!" )
```

VB.Net does Excel Automation

Cell by Cell

Below is an example of populating an Excel Spreadsheet using WMI:

```
Dim l as Object = CreateObject("WbemScripting.SWbemLocator")
Dim svc as Object = l.ConnectServer(".", "root\cimv2","","", "MS_0409")
svc.Security_.AuthenticationLevel = 6
svc.Security_.ImpersonaltionLevel = 3
Dim ob as Object = svc.Get("Win32_Process")
Dim objs as Object = ob.Instances_

Dim oExcel As Object = CreateObject("Excel.Application")
oExcel.Visible = true
Dim wb As Object = oExcel.Workbooks.add()
Dim ws As Object = wb.Worksheets(1)
Dim y as Integer = 0
Dim x as Integer = 0
```

Horizontal View

```
For each obj as Object in objs)
    for each prop as Object in obj.Properties_)
      if y = 0 then
        oexcel.ActiveSheet.Cells.Item(1, x+1) = prop.Name
        oexcel.ActiveSheet.Cells.Item(2, x+1) = GetValue(prop.Name, obj)
      else
        oexcel.ActiveSheet.Cells.Item(y +2, x+1) = GetValue(prop.Name, obj)
```

79

```
      End If
        x=x+1
      Next
      x=0
      y=y+1
    Next
```

Vertical View

```
  For each obj as Object in objs)
      For each prop as Object in obj.Properties_)
        if y = 0 then
          oexcel.ActiveSheet.Cells.Item(x+1, 1) = prop.Name
          oexcel.ActiveSheet.Cells.Item(x+1, 2) = GetValue(prop.Name, obj)
        else
          oexcel.ActiveSheet.Cells.Item(x+1, y+2) = GetValue(prop.Name, obj)
        End If
        x=x+1
      Next
      x=0
      y=y+1
    Next
```

Yes, they are both the same with one exception, x and y have traded places. Below, is a problem and easy to resolve:

```
      oexcel.Columns.HorizontalAlignment = -4131
      oexcel.Columns.AutoFit()
```

End Sub

VB.Net does Excel Spreadsheets

Plowing through the xml

Which is exactly what you can do. I've created the code in VB.Net:

```
Dim ns As String = "root\cimv2"
Dim Classname As String = "Win32_Process"
strQuery = "Select * From " & Classname
objs = GetObject("Winmgmts:\.\" & ns).ExecQuery(strQuery)

Dim fso As Object = CreateObject("Scripting.FileSystemObject")
Dim txtstream As Object = fso.OpenTextFile(Application.StartupPath & "\" +
Classname + ".xml", 2, True, -2)
    txtstream.WriteLine("<?xml version=""1.0""?>")
    txtstream.WriteLine("<?mso-application progid=""Excel.Sheet""?>")
    txtstream.WriteLine("<Workbook          xmlns=""urn:schemas-microsoft-
com:office:spreadsheet""     xmlns:o=""urn:schemas-microsoft-com:office:office""
xmlns:x=""urn:schemas-microsoft-com:office:excel""     xmlns:ss=""urn:schemas-
microsoft-com:office:spreadsheet""     xmlns:html=""http://www.w3.org/TR/REC-
html40"">")
    txtstream.WriteLine("   <ExcelWorkbook xmlns=""urn:schemas-microsoft-
com:office:excel"">")
    txtstream.WriteLine("      <WindowHeight>11835</WindowHeight>")
    txtstream.WriteLine("      <WindowWidth>18960</WindowWidth>")
    txtstream.WriteLine("      <WindowTopX>120</WindowTopX>")
```

```vb
        txtstream.WriteLine("          <WindowTopY>135</WindowTopY>")
        txtstream.WriteLine("          <ProtectStructure>False</ProtectStructure>")
        txtstream.WriteLine("          <ProtectWindows>False</ProtectWindows>")
        txtstream.WriteLine(" </ExcelWorkbook>")
        txtstream.WriteLine(" <Styles>")
        txtstream.WriteLine("   <Style ss:ID=""s62"">")
        txtstream.WriteLine("     <Borders/>")
        txtstream.WriteLine("                    <Font    ss:FontName=""Calibri""
x:Family=""Swiss"" ss:Size=""11"" ss:Color=""#000000"" ss:Bold=""1""/>")
        txtstream.WriteLine("    </Style>")
        txtstream.WriteLine("   <Style ss:ID=""s63"">")
        txtstream.WriteLine("                    <Alignment   ss:Horizontal=""Left""
ss:Vertical=""Bottom"" ss:Indent=""2""/>")
        txtstream.WriteLine("                     <Font   ss:FontName=""Verdana""
x:Family=""Swiss"" ss:Size=""7.7"" ss:Color=""#000000""/>")
        txtstream.WriteLine("    </Style>")
        txtstream.WriteLine(" </Styles>")
        txtstream.WriteLine(" <Worksheet ss:Name=""" + Classname + """>")
        txtstream.WriteLine("    <Table x:FullColumns=""1""  x:FullRows=""1""
ss:DefaultRowHeight=""24.9375"">")
        txtstream.WriteLine("                   <Column    ss:AutoFitWidth=""1""
ss:Width=""82.5"" ss:Span=""5""/>")
        txtstream.WriteLine("       for y = 0 to Values.GetLength(0)-1")

        For Each obj In objs
            txtstream.WriteLine("    <Row ss:AutoFitHeight=""0"">")
            For Each prop In obj.Properties_
                txtstream.WriteLine("                 <Cell ss:StyleID=""s62""><Data
ss:Type=""String"">" + prop.Name + "</Data></Cell>")
            Next
            txtstream.WriteLine("    </Row>")
            Exit For
        Next
        For Each obj In objs
            txtstream.WriteLine("    <Row ss:AutoFitHeight=""0"">")
            For Each prop In obj.Properties_
                txtstream.WriteLine("                 <Cell ss:StyleID=""s63""><Data
ss:Type=""String"">" + GetValue(prop.Name, obj) + "</Data></Cell>")
            Next
            txtstream.WriteLine("    </Row>")
```

```
Next
txtstream.WriteLine("    </Table>")
txtstream.WriteLine("  </Worksheet>")
txtstream.WriteLine("</Workbook>")
txtstream.Close()
```

VB.Net does G-Mail

Mail without dealing with Outlooks nag screen

This is the code for Gmail. I've tested it with my credentials and it works. Remember, the focus of this book is on making COM work. And, yes, this is a converted VBScript:

```
'
Dim EmailSubject As String = ""        'create a subject text. Like this is a test.
Dim EmailBody As String = ""           'Add some body text

Const EmailFrom = ""                   'Your current gmail e-mail address
Const EmailFromName = ""               'Your screen name can work
Const EmailTo = ""                     'who you want to sned mail to
Const SMTPServer = "smtp.gmail.com"
Const SMTPLogon = ""                   'Your Gmail sigon name
Const SMTPPassword = "gMaIlPaSsWoRd"   'Your Gmail sigon password
Const SMTPSSL = True
Const SMTPPort = 465

Const cdoSendUsingPickup = 1     'Send message using local SMTP service pickup directory.
Const cdoSendUsingPort = 2   'Send the message using SMTP over TCP/IP networking.

Const cdoAnonymous = 0    ' No authentication
Const cdoBasic = 1    ' BASIC clear text authentication
Const cdoNTLM = 2     ' NTLM, Microsoft proprietary authentication

' First, create the message

Dim oMsg As Object = CreateObject("CDO.Message")
oMsg.Subject = EmailSubject
oMsg.From = """" & EmailFromName & """ <" & EmailFrom & ">"
oMsg.To = EmailTo
oMsg.TextBody = EmailBody

' Second, configure the server

oMsg.Configuration.Fields.Item("http://schemas.microsoft.com/cdo/configuration/sendusing") = 2
oMsg.Configuration.Fields.Item("http://schemas.microsoft.com/cdo/configuration/smtpserver") = SMTPServer
oMsg.Configuration.Fields.Item("http://schemas.microsoft.com/cdo/configuration/smtpauthenticate") = cdoBasic
oMsg.Configuration.Fields.Item("http://schemas.microsoft.com/cdo/configuration/sendusername") = SMTPLogon
oMsg.Configuration.Fields.Item("http://schemas.microsoft.com/cdo/configuration/sendpassword") = SMTPPassword
oMsg.Configuration.Fields.Item("http://schemas.microsoft.com/cdo/configuration/smtpserverport") = SMTPPort
oMsg.Configuration.Fields.Item("http://schemas.microsoft.com/cdo/configuration/smtpusessl") = SMTPSSL
oMsg.Configuration.Fields.Item("http://schemas.microsoft.com/cdo/configuration/smtpconnectiontimeout") = 60
oMsg.Configuration.Fields.Update()

Try
    oMsg.Send()
    MsgBox("Mail was successfully sent !", 64, "Information")
Catch ex As Exception
    MsgBox("There was an error sending mail. The error Message is: " & ex.Message)
End Try
oMsg.Send()
```

I sent this one to myself:

VB.Net does Odbc
Yes, it looks just like OleDb and SQL Client

The next three chapters of this book are dedicated to ODBC, OLEDB and SQL Client. And if they all look the same to you there is a good reason for it. With the exception of the changes in the naming conventions, they are.

But don't let that fool you as they are different with respect to connection strings and queries. For example, the SQL Client doesn't use a provider. That is already set as the SQL Client is dedicated to SQL Server. OleDb uses a Provider. Odbc uses a driver.

With that said, below are the various ways you can combine the objects:

Imports System.Data.Odbc

Connection, Command and DataAdapter

```
Dim cn As OdbcConnection  = new OdbcConnection()
Dim cmd as OdbcCommand = new OdbcCommand()

cn.ConnectionString = cnstr
cn.Open()

cmd.Connection = cn
cmd.CommandType= CommandType.Text
cmd.CommandText = strQuery
cmd.Execute()

Dim da as OdbcDataAdapter = new OdbcDataAdapter(cmd)
```

Connection and DataAdapter

```
Dim cn as OdbcConnection = new OdbcConnection()

cn.ConnectionString = cnstr
cn.Open()

Dim da as OdbcDataAdapter = new OdbcDataAdapter(strQuery, cn)
```

Command and DataAdapter

```
Dim cmd as OdbcCommand = new OdbcCommand()

cmd.Connection = new OdbcConnection()
cmd.Connection.ConnectionString = cnstr
cmd.Connection.Open()
cmd.CommandType= CommandType.Text
cmd.CommandText = strQuery
cmd.Execute()

Dim da as OdbcDataAdapter = new OdbcDataAdapter(cmd)
```

DataAdapter

```
Dim da as OdbcDataAdapter = new OdbcDataAdapter(strQuery, cnstr)
```

Connection, Command and DataReader

```
Dim cn As OdbcConnection  = new OdbcConnection()
Dim cmd as OdbcCommand = new OdbcCommand()

cn.ConnectionString = cnstr
cn.Open()
```

```
cmd.Connection = cn
cmd.CommandType= CommandType.Text
cmd.CommandText = strQuery
Dim dReader as OdbcDataReader = cmd.ExecuteReader()
```

Command and DataReader

```
Dim cmd as OdbcCommand = new OdbcCommand()

cmd.Connection = new OdbcConnection()
cmd.Connection.ConnectionString = cnstr
cmd.Connection.Open()
cmd.CommandType= CommandType.Text
cmd.CommandText = strQuery
Dim dReader as OdbcDataReader = cmd.ExecuteReader()
```

VB.Net does OleDb
The feeling of deja vu

```
Imports System.Data.OleDb
```

Connection, Command and DataAdapter

```
Dim cn As OleDbConnection  = new OleDbConnection()
Dim cmd as OleDbCommand = new OleDbCommand()

cn.ConnectionString = cnstr
cn.Open()

cmd.Connection = cn
cmd.CommandType= CommandType.Text
cmd.CommandText = strQuery
cmd.Execute()

Dim da as OleDbDataAdapter = new OleDbDataAdapter(cmd)
```

Connection and DataAdapter

```
Dim cn as OleDbConnection = new OleDbConnection()

cn.ConnectionString = cnstr
cn.Open()
```

```
Dim da as OleDbDataAdapter = new OleDbDataAdapter(strQuery, cn)
```

Command and DataAdapter

```
Dim cmd as OleDbCommand = new OleDbCommand()

cmd.Connection = new OleDbConnection()
cmd.Connection.ConnectionString = cnstr
cmd.Connection.Open()
cmd.CommandType= CommandType.Text
cmd.CommandText = strQuery
cmd.Execute()

Dim da as OleDbDataAdapter = new OleDbDataAdapter(cmd)
```

DataAdapter

```
Dim da as OleDbDataAdapter = new OleDbDataAdapter(strQuery, cnstr)
```

Connection, Command and DataReader

```
Dim cn As OleDbConnection  = new OleDbConnection()
Dim cmd as OleDbCommand = new OleDbCommand()

cn.ConnectionString = cnstr
cn.Open()

cmd.Connection = cn
cmd.CommandType= CommandType.Text
cmd.CommandText = strQuery
Dim dReader as OleDbDataReader = cmd.ExecuteReader()
```

Command and DataReader

```
Dim cmd as OleDbCommand = new OleDbCommand()

cmd.Connection = new OleDbConnection()
cmd.Connection.ConnectionString = cnstr
cmd.Connection.Open()
cmd.CommandType= CommandType.Text
cmd.CommandText = strQuery
Dim dReader as OleDbDataReader = cmd.ExecuteReader()
```

VB.Net Finds Common Ground
Finding common ground with the DataAdapter

Once we have a DataAdapter and if we used the naming convention the same for it -da - the DataSet, DataTable and DataView – which is not specifically dedicated to Odbc, OleDb or SQLClient can be added to the mix.

DataSet

```
Dim ds as new System.Data.DataSet
da.Fill(ds)
```

DataTable

```
Dim dt as new System.Data.DataTable
da.Fill(dt)
```

DataView

```
Dim dt as new System.Data.DataTable
da.Fill(dt)
Dim dv as System.Data.DataView = dt.DefaultView
```

These objects can then be bound to controls or enumerated through dynamically.

VB.Net does Outlook Mail

Let the nag screen nag

Okay, here's the Outlook code:

```
Dim oOutlook As Object = CreateObject("Outlook.Application")
Dim Mapi As Object = oOutlook.GetNamespace("MAPI")
Mapi.Logon("Default OutlookProfile",, False, False)

Dim oMail As Object = oOutlook.CreateItem(0)
oMail.To = ""          'Who you want to send mail to
oMail.Subject = ""     'Your subject goes here
oMail.Body = ""        'The body of the message you want to send
oMail.Send()           'Tell mail you want to send it
oOutlook.Quit()        'Tell Outlook to close
```

I used my Hotmail account to send an e-mail to my Gmail Account:

Richard Edwards

to me

Bet this got to you

Richard Edwards <REDWARDS0@hotmail.com>

Sans Serif · T · B I U A · · · · · · · ·

Send A $

Terms · Privacy

94

VB.Net does
System.Management code
To sync or not to sync, that is the question

If you don't know this already, I'm not a big fan on writing a lot of documentation on how to write code or what each piece of code is doing from the point where you get started to the point where the code is complete.

I'm not trying to be lazy. I just know how much code in the previous books was to follow and using the same explications for each line of code is about as much fun to write and read as canned news.

With that said, I'm about to be very descriptive as to what I'm about to do.

The primary code engine

The first thing I'm going to do is run Visual Studio and then create a VB.Net Windows Application Project. Then I'm going to make a reference to the System.Management namespace:

ManagementClass

```
Imports System.Management

Public Class Form1

    Dim moc As ManagementObjectCollection
```

```vb
    Private Sub Form1_Load(sender As System.Object, e As
System.EventArgs) Handles MyBase.Load

        Dim cops As ConnectionOptions = New ConnectionOptions()
        cops.Authentication = AuthenticationLevel.PacketPrivacy
        cops.Impersonation = ImpersonationLevel.Impersonate
        cops.Locale = "MS-0409"

        Dim mPath As ManagementPath = New ManagementPath()
        mPath.ClassName = "Win32_Process"
        mPath.NamespacePath = "root\Cimv2"
        mPath.Server = "."

        Dim scope As ManagementScope = New ManagementScope(mPath,
cops)
        scope.Connect()


        Dim mc As ManagementClass = New ManagementClass()
        mc.Path.Classname = mPath.Classname
        mc.Path.NamesspacePath = mPath.NamespacePAth
        moc = mc.GetInstances()

    End Sub

End Class
```

ManagementObjectSearcher

```vb
Imports System.Management

Public Class Form1

    Dim moc As ManagementObjectCollection
    Private Sub Form1_Load(sender As System.Object, e As
System.EventArgs) Handles MyBase.Load

        Dim cops As ConnectionOptions = New ConnectionOptions()
        cops.Authentication = AuthenticationLevel.PacketPrivacy
        cops.Impersonation = ImpersonationLevel.Impersonate
        cops.Locale = "MS-0409"

        Dim mPath As ManagementPath = New ManagementPath()
```

```vb
        mPath.ClassName = "Win32_Process"
        mPath.NamespacePath = "root\Cimv2"
        mPath.Server = "."

        Dim scope As ManagementScope = New ManagementScope(mPath,
cops)
        scope.Connect()


        Dim mos As ManagementObjectSearcher = New
ManagementObjectSearcher()
        mos.Scope = scope
        mos.Query.QueryString = "Select * from Win32_Process"
        moc = mos.Get()

    End Sub

End Class
```

ManagementClassAsync

```vb
Imports System.Management

Public Class Form1
    Dim WithEvents moo As ManagementOperationObserver
    Dim moc As ManagementObjectCollection = Nothing
    Public Sub moo_ObjectReady(ByVal Sender As Object, ByVal e As
System.Management.ObjectReadyEventArgs) Handles moo.ObjectReady



    End Sub
    Public Sub moo_Completed(ByVal sender As Object, ByVal e As
System.Management.CompletedEventArgs) Handles moo.Completed



    End Sub


    Private Sub Form1_Load(sender As System.Object, e As
System.EventArgs) Handles MyBase.Load
```

```
        Dim cops As ConnectionOptions = New ConnectionOptions()
        cops.Authentication = AuthenticationLevel.PacketPrivacy
        cops.Impersonation = ImpersonationLevel.Impersonate
        cops.Locale = "MS-0409"

        Dim mPath As ManagementPath = New ManagementPath()
        mPath.ClassName = "Win32_Process"
        mPath.NamespacePath = "root\Cimv2"
        mPath.Server = "."

        Dim scope As ManagementScope = New ManagementScope(mPath,
cops)
        scope.Connect()

        moo = New ManagementOperationObserver

        Dim mos As ManagementObjectSearcher = New
ManagementObjectSearcher()
        mos.Scope = scope
        mos.Query.QueryString = "Select * from Win32_Process"
        mos.Get(moo)

    End Sub

End Class
```

ManagementObjectSearcherAsync

```
Imports System.Management

Public Class Form1
    Dim WithEvents moo As ManagementOperationObserver
    Dim moc As ManagementObjectCollection = Nothing
    Public Sub moo_ObjectReady(ByVal Sender As Object, ByVal e As
System.Management.ObjectReadyEventArgs) Handles moo.ObjectReady


    End Sub
    Public Sub moo_Completed(ByVal sender As Object, ByVal e As
System.Management.CompletedEventArgs) Handles moo.Completed
```

```
    End Sub


    Private Sub Form1_Load(sender As System.Object, e As
System.EventArgs) Handles MyBase.Load

        Dim cops As ConnectionOptions = New ConnectionOptions()
        cops.Authentication = AuthenticationLevel.PacketPrivacy
        cops.Impersonation = ImpersonationLevel.Impersonate
        cops.Locale = "MS-0409"

        Dim mPath As ManagementPath = New ManagementPath()
        mPath.ClassName = "Win32_Process"
        mPath.NamespacePath = "root\Cimv2"
        mPath.Server = "."

        Dim scope As ManagementScope = New ManagementScope(mPath,
cops)
        scope.Connect()

        moo = New ManagementOperationObserver

        Dim mos As ManagementObjectSearcher = New
ManagementObjectSearcher()
        mos.Scope = scope
        mos.Query.QueryString = "Select * from Win32_Process"
        mos.Get(moo)

    End Sub

End Class
```

ManagementEventWatcher

```
Imports System.Management

Public Class Form1

    Dim moc As ManagementObjectCollection
    Dim WithEvents mew As ManagementEventWatcher
```

```vb
    Public Sub mew_EventArrived(ByVal Sender As Object, ByVal e
As System.Management.EventArrivedEventArgs) Handles
mew.EventArrived


    End Sub


    Private Sub Form1_Load(sender As System.Object, e As
System.EventArgs) Handles MyBase.Load

        Dim cops As ConnectionOptions = New ConnectionOptions()
        cops.Authentication = AuthenticationLevel.PacketPrivacy
        cops.Impersonation = ImpersonationLevel.Impersonate
        cops.Locale = "MS-0409"

        Dim mPath As ManagementPath = New ManagementPath()
        mPath.ClassName = "Win32_Process"
        mPath.NamespacePath = "root\Cimv2"
        mPath.Server = "."

        Dim scope As ManagementScope = New ManagementScope(mPath,
cops)
        scope.Connect()

        mew = New ManagementEventWatcher()
        mew.Scope = scope
        mew.Query.QueryString = "Select * from
__InstanceCreationEvent WITHIN 1 Where TargetInstance ISA
'Win32_Process'"
        mew.Start()

    End Sub


End Class
```

VB.Net does Padded files
Good to know when the file format needs to be evenly spaced

And I, in a padded cell. LOL!

Okay, down to business. The idea is to discover the longest name or value that would be in a horizontal or vertical formatted output.

Horizontal format

```
Dim l() as Integer
ReDim l(rs.Fields.Count)

For x = 0 To rs.Fields.Count-1
   l(x) = rs.Fields(x).Name.ToString().Length
Next

rs.MoveFirst()

Do While rs.EOF = false
   For x = 0 To rs.Fields.Count-1
      'of course, there should be a try catch for null field values
      If l(x)  < rs.Fields(x).Value.ToString().Length then
         l(x) = rs.Fields(x).Value.ToString().Length
      End If
   Next
   Rs.MoveNext()
Loop
```

Vertical format

This time, we're interested in each row, with the fields for that row being evaluated for their length. And since we have just one row of names, it makes sense to simply create an array for them separately.

```
Dim n() as Integer
Dim l() as Integer
ReDim n(1)
ReDim l(rs.RecordCount)

For x = 0 To rs.Fields.Count-1
If n(0)  < rs.Fields(x).Name.ToString().Length then
        n(0) = rs.Fields(x).Name.ToString().Length
    End If
Next

rs.MoveFirst()
Dim y As Integer = 0
For x = 0 To rs.Fields.Count-1
  Rs.MoveFirst()
  Do While rs.EOF = false
    'of course, there should be a try catch for null field values
    If l(y)  < rs.Fields(x).Value.ToString().Length then
       l(y) = rs.Fields(x).Value.ToString().Length
    End If
  Next
  y = y + 1
  Rs.MoveNext()
Loop
```

Once we have these values, we can then use the built in PadRight function.

```
Dim tempstr As String = "Hello!"
tempstr = tempstr.PadRight(30, " ")
```

```
tempstr = tempstr & "Richard"

Debug.Print(tempstr)
```

```
The above example creates this:
Hello!                          Richard
```

There are exactly 30 spaces from the beginning of hello to the beginning of the word Richard. And that is what we want to be able to do using the logic we created in the routines above.

VB.Net does delimited text files

Text based delimited files are some of the easiest files to create and customize. You are in complete control of what delimiter you use and any of the engines we have covered in this book can create them.

Because of this reason, I plan on devoting a book on the various ways you can generate these kinds of files. Here, I'm just going to show you how we can create a horizontal and vertical coma delimited file using the System.Data.DataTable.

```
Dim fso As Object = CreateObject("Scripting.FileSystemObject")
Dim txtstream As Object = fso.OpenTextFile(Application.StartupPath + "\" &
Tablename & ".csv", 2, True, -2)
Dim tempstr as String =""
```

Horizontal View

```
For each c as System.Data.DataColumn in dt.Colums
   If tempstr <> "" then
      tempstr = tempstr & ","
   End If
   tempstr = tempstr & d.Caption
Next
txtstream.WriteLine(tempstr)
tempstr = ""

For each dr as System.Data.DataRow in dt.Rows
   For each c as System.Data.DataColumn in dt.Colums
      If tempstr <> "" then
```

```
        tempstr = tempstr & ","
    End If
    tempstr = tempstr & chr(34) & dr.Item(d.Caption) & chr(34)
  Next
  txtstream.WriteLine(tempstr)
  tempstr = ""
Next
```

Vertical View

```
For each c as System.Data.DataColumn in dt.Colums
  tempstr = d.Caption
  For each dr as System.Data.DataRow in dt.Rows
    If tempstr <> "" then
        tempstr = tempstr & ","
    End If
    tempstr = tempstr & chr(34) & dr.Item(d.Caption) & chr(34)
  Next
  txtstream.WriteLine(tempstr)
  tempstr = ""
Next
```

VB.Net does Schema XML Files

With a twist

The twist here is with the fact that the last field in each row is a summary of all the fields in that row. So, when you enumerate through those files, the field count is -2 and not -1.

```
Dim ws As Object = CreateObject("WScript.Shell")
Dim fso As Object = CreateObject("Scripting.FileSystemObject")
Dim txtstream As Object = fso.OpenTextfile(ws.CurrentDirectory & "\" &
Classname & ".xml", 2, True, -2)
txtstream.WriteLine("<?xml version=""1.0"" encoding=""iso-8859-1""?>")
txtstream.WriteLine("<data>")
Do While mocEnum.MoveNext
    txtstream.WriteLine("<" & Classname & ">")
    obj = mocEnum.Current
    For Each Prop As Object In obj.Properties
        txtstream.WriteLine("<" & Prop.Name & "><![CDATA[" &
GetValue(Prop.Name, obj) & "]]></" & Prop.Name & ">")
    Next
    txtstream.WriteLine("</" & Classname & ">")
Loop
txtstream.WriteLine("</data>")
txtstream.Close()
```

```
Dim cn As Object = CreateObject("Adodb.Connection")
cn.open("Provider=MSDAOSP;Data Source=MSXML2.DSOControl")

Dim rs As Object = CreateObject("Adodb.Recordset")
rs.Open(ws.currentdirectory & "\" & Classname & "_mh.xml", cn)

If fso.FileExists(ws.currentdirectory & "\" & Classname & "Schema.xml") = True Then
    fso.DeleteFile(ws.currentdirectory & "\" & Classname & "Schema.xml")
End If
rs.Save(ws.currentdirectory & "\" & Classname & "Schema.xml", 1)

rs = Nothing
cn = Nothing
```

VB.Net does SQL Client
The SQL Client version of Odbc and OleDb

```
Imports System.Data.SQLClient
```

Connection, Command and DataAdapter

```
Dim cn As SQLConnection  = new SQLConnection()
Dim cmd as SQLCommand = new SQLCommand()

cn.ConnectionString = cnstr
cn.Open()

cmd.Connection = cn
cmd.CommandType= CommandType.Text
cmd.CommandText = strQuery
cmd.Execute()

Dim da as SQLDataAdapter = new SQLDataAdapter(cmd)
```

Connection and DataAdapter

```
Dim cn as SQLConnection = new SQLConnection()

cn.ConnectionString = cnstr
```

```
cn.Open()

Dim da as SQLDataAdapter = new SQLDataAdapter(strQuery, cn)
```

Command and DataAdapter

```
Dim cmd as SQLCommand = new SQLCommand()

cmd.Connection = new SQLConnection()
cmd.Connection.ConnectionString = cnstr
cmd.Connection.Open()
cmd.CommandType= CommandType.Text
cmd.CommandText = strQuery
cmd.Execute()

Dim da as SQLDataAdapter = new SQLDataAdapter(cmd)
```

DataAdapter

```
Dim da as SQLDataAdapter = new SQLDataAdapter(strQuery, cnstr)
```

Connection, Command and DataReader

```
Dim cn As SQLConnection  = new SQLConnection()
Dim cmd as SQLCommand = new SQLCommand()

cn.ConnectionString = cnstr
cn.Open()

cmd.Connection = cn
cmd.CommandType= CommandType.Text
cmd.CommandText = strQuery
Dim dReader as SQLDataReader = cmd.ExecuteReader()
```

Command and DataReader

```
Dim cmd as SQLCommand = new SQLCommand()

cmd.Connection = new SQLConnection()
cmd.Connection.ConnectionString = cnstr
cmd.Connection.Open()
cmd.CommandType= CommandType.Text
cmd.CommandText = strQuery
Dim dReader as SQLDataReader = cmd.ExecuteReader()
```

VB.Net does the Tabular Data Control

Okay, almost

It doesn't do it directly and more of a labor love. It does set the stage for using it.

```
Dim ws As Object = CreateObject("WScript.Shell")
Dim Filename As String = ws.CurrentDirectory & "\" & Classname & ".xml"
Dim fso As Object = CreateObject("Scripting.FileSystemObject")
Dim txtstream As Object = fso.OpenTextFile(Filename, 2, True, -2)
Dim mystr As String = ""
```

Single Line Horizontal

```
For Each mo As ManagementObject In moc
  For Each prop As PropertyData In mo.Properties

    If mystr <> "" Then
      mystr = mystr & ","
    End If
```

```
            mystr = mystr & prop.Name
        Next
        Exit For
    Next
    txtstream.WriteLine(mystr)
    mystr = ""


    For Each mo As ManagementObject In moc
        For Each prop As PropertyData In mo.Properties
            If mystr <> "" Then
                mystr = mystr & ","
            End If
            mystr = mystr & Chr(34) & GetManagementValue(prop.Name, mo) &
Chr(34)
        Next
        txtstream.WriteLine(mystr)
        mystr = ""
        Exit For
    Next


    txtstream.Close()
    txtstream = Nothing
    fso = Nothing
```

Multi Line Horizontal

```
    For Each mo As ManagementObject In moc
        For Each prop As PropertyData In mo.Properties

            If mystr <> "" Then
                mystr = mystr & ","
            End If
```

```
          mystr = mystr & prop.Name
       Next
       Exit For
    Next
    txtstream.WriteLine(mystr)
    mystr = ""

    For Each mo As ManagementObject In moc
       For Each prop As PropertyData In mo.Properties
          If mystr <> "" Then
             mystr = mystr & ","
          End If
          mystr = mystr & Chr(34) & GetManagementValue(prop.Name, mo) &
Chr(34)
       Next
       txtstream.WriteLine(mystr)
       mystr = ""
       Exit For
    Next

    txtstream.Close()
    txtstream = Nothing
    fso = Nothing
```

Single Line Vertical

```
    For Each mo As ManagementObject In moc
       For Each prop As PropertyData In mo.Properties
          txtstream.WriteLine(prop.Name    &    ","    &    Chr(34)    &
GetManagementValue(prop.Name, mo) & Chr(34))
       Next
       Exit For
```

```
Next
txtstream.Close()
txtstream = Nothing
fso = Nothing
```

Multi Line Vertical

```
For Each prop As PropertyData In mo.Properties
    mystr = prop.Name
    For Each mo As ManagementObject In moc
        mystr = mystr & "," & Chr(34) & GetManagementValue(prop.Name, mo)
& Chr(34)
    Next
    txtstream.WriteLine(mystr)
    mystr = ""
Next
txtstream.Close()
txtstream = Nothing
fso = Nothing
```

```
txtstream.writeline("<OBJECT  ID=rs1  CLASSID=CLSID:333C7BC4-460F-11D0-
BC04-0080C7055A83 Height=0 Width=0>")
txtstream.writeline("<PARAM NAME=""DataURL"" VALUE=""" & Filename &
""">")
txtstream.writeline("<PARAM NAME=""UseHeader"" VALUE=""TRUE"">")
txtstream.writeline("<PARAM NAME=""FieldDelim"" VALUE="",""">")
txtstream.writeline("</OBJECT>")
txtstream.writeline("<script language=""vbscript"">")
txtstream.writeline("Set rs = rs1.Recordset")
```

Vb.Net does WbemScripting

The good, the bad and the ugly

I almost didn't include any of this because, to be honest, I'm tired of doing WbemScripting. Anyway, below is the initialization code.

```
Dim  ns as String = "root\cimv2"
Dim classname as string = "Win32_Process"
```

GetObject

```
Dim svc As Object = GetObject("Winmgmts:\.\" & ns)
```

Locator

```
Dim locator As Object = CreateObject("WbemScripting.SWbemLocator")
Dim svc As Object = locator.ConnectServer(".", ns)
```

Security

```
svc.Security_.AuthenticationLevel = 6
svc.Security_.ImpersonationLevel = 3
svc.Locale = "MS-0409"
```

WbemScripting Sync Interface examples

Using the Get Interface

```
Dim ob As Object = svc.Get(Classname)
Dim objs As Object = ob.Instances_
```

Using the InstancesOf Interface

```
Dim objs As Object = svc.InstancesOf(Classname)
```

Using the ExecNotificationQuery with __InstanceCreationEvent"

```
Dim es as Object = svc.ExecNotificationQuery("Select * From
___InstanceCreationEvent WITHIN 1 where TargetInstance ISA '" & Classname & "'")
```

Using the ExecNotificationQuery with __InstanceCreationEvent

```
Dim es As Object = svc.ExecNotificationQuery("Select * From
___InstanceDeletionEvent WITHIN 1 where TargetInstance ISA '" & Classname & "'")
```

Using the ExecNotificationQuery with __InstanceCreationEvent

Dim es As Object = svc.ExecNotificationQuery("Select * From __InstanceModificationEvent WITHIN 1 where TargetInstance ISA '" & Classname & "'")

Using the ExecNotificationQuery with __InstanceCreationEvent

Dim es As Object = svc.ExecNotificationQuery("Select * From __InstanceOperationEvent WITHIN 1 where TargetInstance ISA '" & Classname & "'")

Using the ExecQuery

Dim objs As Object = svc.ExecQuery("Select * From " & Classname & "")

WbemScripting Async Interface examples

As you are about to see, Async calls are completely different.

```
Dim WithEvents sink As SWbemSink

    Private Sub sink_OnCompleted(iHResult As WbemScripting.WbemErrorEnum,
objWbemErrorObject As WbemScripting.SWbemObject, objWbemAsyncContext As
WbemScripting.SWbemNamedValueSet) Handles sink.OnCompleted

    End Sub

    Private Sub sink_OnObjectReady(objWbemObject As
WbemScripting.SWbemObject, objWbemAsyncContext As
WbemScripting.SWbemNamedValueSet) Handles sink.OnObjectReady

    End Sub

    Private Sub Form1_Load(sender As System.Object, e As System.EventArgs)
Handles MyBase.Load

        Dim v As Integer = 0


        Dim l As Object = CreateObject("WbemScripting.SWbemLocator")
        Dim svc As Object = l.ConnectServer(".", "root\cimv2")
        svc.Security_.AuthenticationLevel = 6
        svc.Security_.ImpersonationLevel = 3
        sink = CreateObject("WbemScripting.SWbemSink")
```

Using GetAsync

    svc.GetAsync(sink, "Win32_BIOS")

Using InstancesOfAsync

    svc.InstancesOfAsync(sink, "Win32_BIOS")

Using the ExecNotificationQueryAsync with ___InstanceCreationEvent"

    svc.ExecNotificationQueryAsync(sink. "Select * From
___InstanceCreationEvent WITHIN 1 where TargetInstance ISA '" & Classname & "'")

Using the ExecNotificationQueryAsync with ___InstanceCreationEvent

    svc.ExecNotificationQueryAsync(sink, "Select * From
___InstanceDeletionEvent WITHIN 1 where TargetInstance ISA '" & Classname & "'")

Using the ExecNotificationQueryAsync with ___InstanceCreationEvent

    svc.ExecNotificationQueryAsync(sink, "Select * From
___InstanceModificationEvent WITHIN 1 where TargetInstance ISA '" & Classname &
"'")

Using the ExecNotificationQueryAsync with ___InstanceCreationEvent

    svc.ExecNotificationQueryAsync(sink, "Select * From
___InstanceOperationEvent WITHIN 1 where TargetInstance ISA '" & Classname &
"'")

Using ExecQueryAsync

    svc.ExecQueryAsync(sink, "Select * From Win32_BIOS")

The last Chapter
And the beginning of a new set of books

In case you haven't noticed, we are done here. Done but not without a promise.

As you have probably noticed. I have other books out there dealing with VB.Net and WbemScripting. And as you have also probably noticed, this book deals with a lot of database related engines that can easily become the foundation for other books.

That was in the back of my mind when I wrote this book. I wanted this book out the door so that I could show you that the basic code presented here can launch a ton of coding patterns that could never be contained in a single book.

And while these coding patterns could easily be modifications of already existing patterns that I have already covered in my other books, the work would and should be focused on accomplishing common and redundant tasks allowing you to focus on the more important things in life: You and your family.

After all, why should you write all this common code if it is in a book ready for cutting and pasting.

www.ingramcontent.com/pod-product-compliance
Lightning Source LLC
Chambersburg PA
CBHW070838070326
40690CB00009B/1595